D1121490

946.08
Davis, Daniel S.
Spain's civil war; the
last great cause

MAR 28
JAN

946.08
Davis, Daniel S.
Spain's civil war; the last gr
great cause

DISCARD

POLSON CITY LIBRARY
Box 820
Polson, Montana 59860

# Spain's Civil War

## THE LAST GREAT CAUSE

# Spain's Civil War

## THE LAST GREAT CAUSE

## by Daniel S. Davis

*illustrated with photographs*

E. P. DUTTON & CO., INC.  NEW YORK

Full credit for painting reproduced on pages 110–111:
PICASSO, Pablo. *Guernica.* (1937, May–early June).
Oil on canvas, 11′ 5½″ x 25′ 5¾″. On extended loan to
The Museum of Modern Art, New York, from the artist.

The lines from Pablo Neruda's "Song to Stalingrad" on
page 64 are reprinted by permission of New Directions
Publishing Corporation, publishers of Pablo Neruda's
*Residence on Earth,* translated by Donald D. Walsh. Copyright © 1973 by Pablo Neruda and Donald D. Walsh.

The lines from W. H. Auden's "Spain 1937" on page 70
are reprinted from *The Collected Poetry of W. H. Auden*
by permission of Random House, Inc. Copyright 1940,
copyright renewal 1968 by W. H. Auden.

*Map by Joan Rhine*

Copyright © 1975 by Daniel S. Davis

All rights reserved. No part of this publication may be
reproduced or transmitted in any form or by any means,
electronic or mechanical, including photocopy, recording,
or any information storage and retrieval system now
known or to be invented, without permission in writing
from the publisher, except by a reviewer who wishes to
quote brief passages in connection with a review written
for inclusion in a magazine, newspaper, or broadcast.

*Library of Congress Cataloging in Publication Data*

Davis, Daniel S.   Spain's civil war; the last great cause.

SUMMARY: Examines the causes, events, and aftermath of
the three-year struggle between the opposing forces
in the Spanish Civil War.

1. Spain—History—Civil War, 1936–1939—Juvenile
literature.   [1. Spain—History—Civil War, 1936–1939]
I. Title.
DP269.D34   946.081   74-7045   ISBN 0-525-39715-9

Published simultaneously in Canada by Clarke,
Irwin & Company Limited, Toronto and Vancouver

*Designed by Meri Shardin*
Printed in the U.S.A.   First Edition
10  9  8  7  6  5  4  3  2  1

*For*
*Julius and Rose*

# Contents

*Photographs appear on pages 107–116.*

# Some Organizations and Political Parties

Carlists: Militant right-wing group. Its extremist Catholic and Monarchist views were rooted in factionalism of the nineteenth-century civil wars. Based in Navarre.

CEDA *Confederación Española de Derechas Autónomas* (National Confederation of Autonomous Rightists): An independent group of Catholic rightist parties led by José María Gil Robles.

CNT *Confederación Nacional de Trabajo* (National Confederation of Labor): Anarchist labor union. Strongest in rural regions and in Barcelona.

FAI *Federación Anarquista Ibérica* (Iberian Anarchist Federation): A revolutionary group that was part of the CNT and politically influential with the rural Anarchist masses.

*Falange Española*: A nationalist political party (with fascist leanings) founded and led by José Antonio Primo de Rivera from 1933 to 1936.

FET y de la JONS *Falange Española Tradicionalista ya de las Juntas de Ofensiva Nacional-Sindicalista*: The only authorized political party in Nationalist Spain, formed in 1937 by General Francisco Franco, who merged the *Falange* with the Carlists.

JONS *Juntas de Ofensiva Nacional-Sindicalista* (National Syndicalist Offensive Junta): Militant political party that fused with the *Falange Española* in 1934.

Popular Front: A coalition of Republican parties, Socialists, and Communists.

POUM *Partido Obrero de Unificación Marxista* (Workers' Party of Marxist Unification): An anti-Stalinist Marxist party.

UGT *Unión General de Trabajadores* (General Workers Union): The trade union of the Socialists, at one time led by Largo Caballero.

UME *Unión Militar Española* (Spanish Military Union): An organization of officers opposed to Manuel Azaña's reforms.

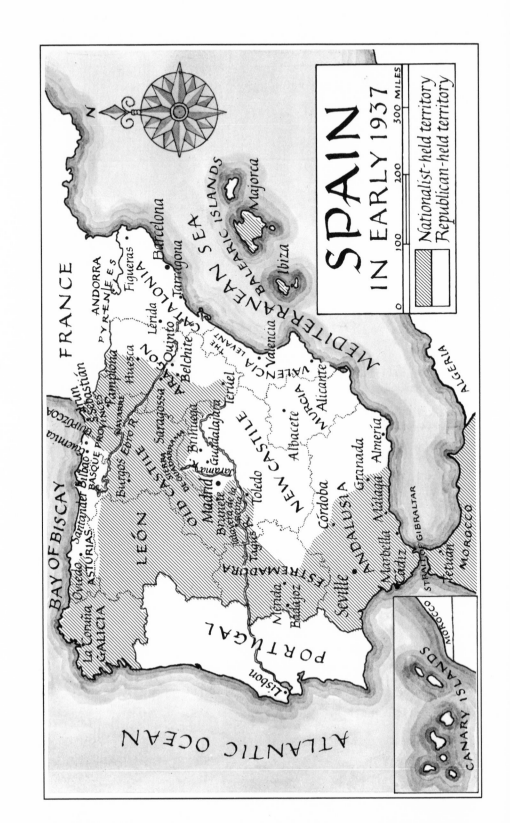

# Introduction

There is a famous old story about the entrance into heaven of Ferdinand III, a sainted thirteenth-century king of Castile. There, he was introduced to the Virgin Mary, who asked him what favors he wished for his beloved land. The king asked first for oil, wine, and corn, and the Virgin granted his wish. He asked for sunny skies, brave men, and pretty women. Again, she said yes. He asked for cigars, relics, garlic, and bulls, and once more she complied. Finally, the monarch asked for good government. "No," said the Virgin, "that can never be granted; for were it bestowed, not an angel would remain a day longer in heaven."

So does myth explain the great riches of the Spanish soil, the virtues of her people, and the misrule that plummeted Spain from its position as the most powerful nation in the world to one of the most backward in western Europe. In modern times Spain has suffered through governments that were incompetent, corrupt, or imposed by foreign powers, and it has been led by kings who were cruel and insane, by narrow-minded military chiefs, and by petty dictators.

But there was one brief period in the dismal story of misrule and oppression by a small, self-serving oligarchy; one small island of hope in Spain's modern political history. In

1931 a republic was established by reformers who sought to open the windows of Spain to the modern world, letting in the fresh, bracing air of freedom, of liberty, and of greater economic justice. The infant Republic was born amid joy and celebration, but it grew sickly and died in a tragic civil war that left the nation in ruins. The agony of that civil war was shared by the whole world, for its bitter battles, in Winston Churchill's words, had "a significance which expands beyond the Spanish peninsula."

It was a war that pitted brother against brother, as all civil wars do. It was a war that was terribly bloody, as most wars are. It was a war of ideas in which each side was incapable of even understanding the basic principles held by its enemies, as most Spanish wars are. It was a war that mobilized the imagination of that part of the world which believed in human dignity and in human equality; a war that, for many, was "the last great cause," the last war in which one could openly believe in ideals worth fighting and dying for.

Like many wars that take place in weak and small nations, it was a war that involved the great powers of the world, who intervened with weapons and soldiers and sought to manipulate the warring factions in order to dominate Spain itself. The Spanish Civil War became the first act of a global tragedy. Spain became the battleground not only of warring Spaniards but of warring ideologies—fascism, communism, and democracy. The poisonous weeds that flourished in Spain's Civil War spread until they covered the world in World War II.

It is that civil war—the war that ended democracy in Spain, the war that left more than a million Spaniards dead and wounded, the war that brought the heavy, brutal hand of misery down upon the necks of the Spanish people—it is the story of that terrible war we shall tell in these pages.

# 1

# *The Republic*

Purple, gold, and red flags were everywhere. Miraculously, it seemed, these Republican colors were suddenly hanging from the windows, balconies, lampposts, autos, and official buildings. They were clutched in the hands of small children and were waved by the students and workers who marched through the streets of Madrid singing the hymn of the French Revolution, the "Marseillaise," and the traditional anthem of the Spanish Republicans, the "Himno de Riego." By nightfall on April 14, 1931, the streets fanning out from the center of the city, the Puerta del Sol, were jammed with thousands upon thousands of Madrileños, their voices lifted in song, in *vivas* for their new government, and in cries of anger against the king, Don Alfonso XIII, the last of the long line of Bourbon monarchs who had ruled Spain—on and off—since 1700. As the joyous throngs catapulted through the streets, as they tore the red and gold flags of royalty, as they chipped away at the stone carvings of royal arms on public buildings—the king, his son, and some of his ministers and assistants piled into three waiting cars and began the long night's journey into exile.

Alfonso's reign had been as long as it had been unhappy for the country. He came to the throne in 1902, when the nation still reeled from the shock of the disastrous loss of its remaining American and Asian colonies to the United States in the Spanish-American War of 1898. The removal of these last vestiges of a once great empire stunned many intellectuals into closer examination of Spanish society. This encouraged the growth of liberal ideas that eventually led to the founding of the Republic.

Spain presented a dismal picture at the turn of the century. Compared with the rest of Europe it was backward, isolated, and impoverished. A popular saying was that "Africa begins at the Pyrenees," Spain's border with France. Political life consisted of the two major parties—the Liberals and the Conservatives—alternating in power through an arrangement to share the spoils of office. Behind the façade of constitutional democracy, the country was ruled by a small group of aristocrats and wealthy landowners. Votes were controlled by the *caciques*—local landowners or their agents, who were like feudal lords of their villages.

The *caciques'* power was enforced by the dreaded Guardia Civil, the national police force that had been created to stop banditry and now served as the government's first line of defense against its own people. From time to time the pent-up anger of the hungry peasants broke loose. Radical gunmen assassinated high political figures and leading churchmen, and once even tried to kill the young king, but such sporadic outbursts of revolutionary violence were ruthlessly put down. Illiteracy and hunger were widespread. In some provinces, such as Catalonia, independence movements thrived. The country's ruling class derived its wealth from the land and failed to encourage industrial growth. Spain exported its agricultural and mineral wealth to other nations, and its landless peasants to its own teeming cities, where they found the urban equivalent of the misery of the countryside.

King Alfonso lived in a cocoon, surrounded by aristocrats, rich landowners, and court favorites. He was cut off from contact with the people and busied himself with meddling in politics and in the army. After the king's interference in army tactics led to a terrible defeat in Spain's colonial war in Morocco that cost the lives of 10,000 soldiers, the unpopular king's throne tottered. A special investigating committee of the Cortes, Spain's parliament, prepared a report condemning the king and his incompetent army, but before it could be released the government was overthrown. The military governor of Catalonia, General Miguel Primo de Rivera, issued a *pronunciamiento*, or announcement of a take-over of the government, in September 1923. With the king's blessings, Primo established a dictatorship in Madrid, suspended the constitution, and dismissed the Cortes.

Primo's regime was successful at first. He ended the long, drawn-out war in Morocco, started a broad program of highway construction and waterworks, and ruled with a firm, though not brutal, hand. But his dictatorship soon became unpopular because many of his measures enraged large sectors of the population. His destruction of the political parties and the continued suspension of the constitution were tolerated as long as Spain's economy thrived, but with the coming of the worldwide Great Depression, discontent with the dictator and his protector, the king, grew. When, in January 1930, Primo's brother officers in the army turned against him, he resigned and went into exile in Paris, where he died a few months later.

Primo left the basic problems of the country untouched. It has been estimated that Spain in 1930 was at the level of development reached by England nearly a century earlier and by France in the 1860's. He left a political vacuum, too, which the king tried to fill with a military-dominated government whose failures brought the country to the brink of revolution. By the end of the year representatives of all factions of anti-Monarchist sentiment, ranging from Conservative businessmen to Socialist activists, agreed to overthrow the king and establish a republic governed by democratically elected representatives of the people.

With rebellion in the air, Alfonso decided to make a last-ditch effort to save his throne by restoring constitutional government. He scheduled elections for municipal offices to test the national mood and to see if it would be safe to return to the political system that existed before Primo's coup. On April 12, 1931, Spaniards voted, and they delivered a crushing blow to the king. The rural, *cacique*-ridden districts, as expected, voted for Monarchist candidates. But in nearly all of Spain's cities, where public opinion was freer, the vote was overwhelmingly for Republican candidates.

While the returns, with their message of impending doom for the king, were trickling in, the last of Spain's Bourbon rulers consulted with his advisers. Royal survival, they decided, depended on the loyalty of the armed forces. When the head of the Guardia Civil, the influential General José Sanjurjo, declared he would not fight to preserve the monarchy, Alfonso did the only thing he could do in a hopeless situation: murmuring, "We are out of fashion," he left the country.

Even as the forlorn king sat huddled with his advisers on the morning of April 14, the Republicans had seized power, and a temporary government headed by Prime Minister Niceto Alcalá Zamora took office amid the deliriously joyous cheers of the swelling crowds in the Puerta del Sol. A mood of hope swept the country as Spaniards called their new Republic *la niña bonita,* "the pretty girl."

Democratic elections were held in June 1931, and the new Cortes, dominated by a coalition of Socialists and moderate Republicans, set to work to draft a new constitution. The leading figure in the new government was Minister of War Manuel Azaña, who became Prime Minister in October. Azaña was an intellectual, a translator, novelist, and literary critic of some repute, whose forceful thinking and brilliant oratory were widely admired. His faults were typically Spanish—a single-mindedness that did not allow room for compromise and an abrasive personality derived from great pride, which helped alienate those who might otherwise have supported him. Azaña's reform program was aimed at making Spain into a democratic, secular state that would reduce the power of the aristocracy, the Church, and the army, and modernize the country for the benefit of the small but growing urban middle class and the peasantry.

These goals were incorporated into a new constitution that passed the Cortes in December 1931, after months of heated debate. It declared Spain a "Republic of workers of all categories," gave the vote to women, provided for a parliamentary democracy with an elected Cortes, placed limits on the powers of the president, and guaranteed the rights of the individual. It also separated Church and state, dissolved the Jesuits and nationalized their property, placed severe limitations on other religious orders, and allowed divorce and civil marriage. These clauses were designed to strip the Church of its special place in the nation, but although similar to measures taken years earlier in other Catholic countries, they aroused deep hostility.

The Catholic Church held a privileged position in Spain. It was the official state religion, received large subsidies from the government, and controlled education in the country. The

hierarchy, often composed of rigid and narrow men, identi-
fied the Church with the monarchy and seemed more concerned with the maintenance of their power than with the
spiritual needs of their flock. Typical of the Church's reactionary leadership was its primate, Cardinal Pedro Segura,
Archbishop of Toledo, who greeted the establishment of the
Republic with a public declaration dripping with nostalgia for
the good old days of Alfonso and urging Catholics to fight
against the new government's efforts to alter the status of the
Church.

Since it was forced to sell its vast landholdings during one
of Spain's recurrent periods of anti-clerical liberal rule in
the 1830's, the Church concentrated its investments in banks,
mining, and industry, and in nearly all forms of business.
Although estimates of Church wealth were grossly exaggerated, there is no doubt that the Church was an ally of the
wealthy and powerful. As a result, it became isolated from
the people and attendance plunged, leading Azaña to claim:
"Spain has ceased to be Catholic."

The rift between the Church and the people erupted into
violence on May 11, 1931, just days after publication of
Cardinal Segura's diatribe against the government. A Jesuit
church in the heart of Madrid was set on fire and a large
crowd, including firemen whose equipment sat idle on the
street, watched the red-yellow tongues of flame lick their way
skyward. Soon, other churches were set ablaze, and by that
afternoon churches in Madrid's suburbs were put to the torch.

The government was slow to react. It feared the prospect
of firing on its own citizens just weeks after deposing the
hated king. "All the covents in Spain are not worth the life
of one Republican," one minister said. But after the violence
spread, the Cabinet relented. By evening troops patrolled
Madrid's empty streets, enforcing the declaration of martial

law. Then, the south erupted. In Málaga forty-one buildings, including the bishop's palace, were burned; in Seville four churches were destroyed; in Alicante, thirteen. The orgy of burning left dozens of churches throughout southern and central Spain in ashes. To this day it is not known whether they were burned by Leftist revolutionaries or by Monarchist extremists out to embarrass the Republic.

The attacks on the churches and the government's slowness to act frightened the middle classes for whom the preservation of order was the first duty of government. And the government's move to close Church-run schools confirmed the worst fears of Catholic Spaniards. The Republic intended to break the Church's educational power, which, it claimed, was a reactionary influence that prevented modernizing reforms. Anti-clerical politicians charged that Church control of schools had led to an illiteracy rate of nearly 50 percent and to a million and a half children being currently out of school. This, they said, showed the Church's indifference to educating the poor. Spain's bishops angrily declared the move a violation of the laws of the Church and ordered the faithful to ignore the government's order.

The Republic's war with the Church may have been necessary for creating a modern society, but it placed believing Catholics in the awkward dilemma of choosing between their government and their Church, alienating many who would otherwise support the Republic. By making church-state relations its top priority, the Republic breathed new life into a dying Church, created a powerful enemy that was to hurry its downfall, and diverted itself from far more important issues in favor of a symbolic battle that strained society to the breaking point.

Azaña was also determined to increase self-government in Spain's provinces. Regional autonomy was an important issue in a country that had once been a collection of independent kingdoms and duchies. After the unification of Spain in the fifteenth century there began a process of "Castilianization," or the economic, cultural, and political domination by the region of Castile. Nowhere was this more resented than in the Basque region and in Catalonia, both of which possessed a sense of separateness and a heritage of history, tradition, and language different from that of the rest of the country. On April 14, 1931, when all Spain was celebrating the birth of the Republic, Catalan leaders were proclaiming a Catalan Republic and spoke of a "federation" with the rest of Spain. So it was urgent that a formula be devised to relax Madrid's rule over these regions.

In 1932 Catalonia won the right to parliamentary self-government in local affairs and equality for the Catalan language. Comparisons are inexact, but the region received powers of self-government that were somewhat less than those enjoyed by state governments in the United States. Even so, this approach to regionalism was bitterly attacked by many Spaniards who resented loosening the centrist tradition that kept Madrid dominant. Meanwhile, demands for regional autonomy were growing in Galicia, in Valencia, and above all, in the Basque region, which approved its own autonomy statute by an overwhelming vote in November 1933.

By backing greater self-government for regions that wanted it, the Azaña regime won popularity in Catalonia and helped reconcile the devoutly Catholic Basques to a national government that was fighting their Church. But the most pressing of Spain's problems, and the one that proved the most intractable, was "the social question"—the unequal distribution of land in an agricultural economy and the widespread poverty that resulted from it.

Spain's economy was based on agriculture; more than two out of three workers were on farms. The south, where nearly a third of Spain's 25 million people lived, was a land of latifundia, huge farms worked by day laborers and usually owned by absentee landlords. It was estimated that only 10,000 families owned half the land in south and central Spain. The latifundia embraced the best farming land, but were often allowed to lie fallow, were used as pasture for cattle, or were simply farmed well below capacity through the indifference of their wealthy owners. Sometimes the land was used to breed fighting bulls or as a game preserve for vacation shooting parties. Profits from country estates went into spending binges in Paris, into Swiss bank accounts, or into buying still more land.

In Andalusia less than 1 percent of the landholders got half of the region's income, leaving the rest to be split among the other 99 percent. Small farmers could not survive without renting themselves out as laborers on the estates; over a million of them made less than a peseta a day from their own holdings. (A peseta was worth about twelve cents during the early 1930's.) Large landowners often rented out their land for farms, or made sharecropping agreements, receiving a portion of the crop as rent. But such arrangements left the tenants and sharecroppers at the mercy of the landlords, to whom they were often deep in debt.

The majority of the south's population neither owned land nor rented it; they were *braceros*, day laborers, who eked out an existence drenched in the squalor of the most extreme poverty in Europe. Their day began with the "slave market," the assembly of unemployed workers at the village square where the landlord's agents would hire the lucky ones for a day's work. If a laborer was known as a troublemaker, either because he was politically active or complained about the low wages, he would not be given work. For much of the year there was no work for anybody; in many districts the average worker was unemployed for well over half the year. When he did work, the *bracero* was paid about forty cents for a back-breaking day in the sun-broiled fields, and women and children were paid even less.

The diseased agricultural economy infected the whole country. Rural poverty meant loss of natural markets for industry, which led to high protective tariffs that kept cheap foreign goods out of the country and kept domestic industry inefficient and high-priced. In the thirty years before the Republic these conditions forced over 2 million Spaniards to emigrate to the Americas in search of a better life. Even more left the countryside in hopes of finding work in the cities, but their lives there were little better and their numbers drove wages down.

An old proverb describes the situation: "In Spain there are two Spains: one that works and does not eat, and the other that eats but does not work." One Spain was dominated by the tightly knit oligarchy that controlled the nation's wealth and was supported by the Church, the army, and a large part of the middle classes, whose jobs, small businesses, and security were dependent on that small group of people. The other Spain, the impoverished workers and unemployed peasants, was ripe for revolution.

Violence was common in the tense countryside. Peasant strikes, land seizures, and barn burnings brought swift vengeance from the hired guns of the landlords and from the trigger-happy Guardia Civil. From time to time the flickering violence flared into bloody outbursts that electrified the country. One of the most brutal incidents came in January 1933

when a revolt at Casas Viejas, in Andalusia, was put down
with extreme harshness. A house in which some militants
barricaded themselves with their children was bombed and
a dozen prisoners were executed in cold blood after the rebellion was ended, their bodies left in the village square as
a lesson to the peasants.

The Casas Viejas incident severely damaged Azaña's government. Not only did a leftist government resort to the brutality of the monarchy, but the outrage was committed by the
Republic's own police arm, the Assault Guards, which was
made up of picked Republicans to avoid reliance on the hated
Guardia for keeping order. Azaña used the emergency powers
he won in the Law for the Defense of the Republic to jail
political offenders and ban and censor newspapers. The law
was aimed at right-wing Monarchists, but was more often used
to cope with the threat from the revolutionary Left. At times,
the army was called out to suppress mass risings, as in the
general strike in Seville during the summer of 1931 in which
thirty people were killed and two hundred wounded.

But force could not solve the problems caused by rural
poverty. Spain needed far-reaching land reforms, but the
Azaña government could not bring itself to inaugurate the
necessary revolutionary measures. It had too great a respect
for private property to seize the latifundia, to set up coopera-
tive farms, or to take other innovative steps. It was too weak
to take the powerful banks away from the oligarchs who ran
them and provide credit to small farmers. The half-measures
it did take, while strong enough to earn the enmity of the
landed classes, were far too inadequate to satisfy the enlarged
expectations of the land-hungry peasants.

The Republic passed a series of laws and decrees to better
conditions for workers and for farm laborers. Wages were

raised and unions were encouraged. An income tax, which might have been used to redistribute the nation's wealth, was passed in 1932, but it provided for only a 1 percent tax on incomes of 100,000 pesetas in a country where the average annual income was about 1,000 pesetas per person. An Agrarian Reform Law took some land for redistribution to farm workers, but very few peasants were actually settled on their own land. The law was so complex and so riddled with legal loopholes that the historian Gabriel Jackson has written: "One would have thought the law written for an association of unemployed lawyers who wished to assure not only their own, but their sons' futures, rather than a law written for the peasants of Spain."

These feeble reforms only whetted the countryside's appetite for more, and drove the landless peasants into Socialist unions that demanded collectivized agriculture and an end to the latifundia system. Others joined Anarchist unions that sought to overthrow the government and institute what they called "libertarian communism," which they defined as "the organization of society without a State and without private property." Spanish Anarchists believed that all men are essentially good and that only their institutions, such as the Church or the government, make men exploit one another. Destroy these institutions, Anarchists believed, and men would come together voluntarily in communes that would cooperate with neighboring communes in a loose federation that would cover all of Spain.

Anarchism spoke to a deep strain within the Spanish character: it appealed to the Spaniard's strong individualism and distrust of authority, to his village-centered traditions, and to that aristocratic streak in his nature that makes the Spanish, no matter how poor and deprived, people of great pride with uncompromising principles, dignity, and honesty. Perhaps that is why the idea of anarchism, founded by Bakunin in the mid-nineteenth century, became a powerful mass movement only in Spain.

For all their idealism, the Anarchists were prone to violence. Their *pistoleros*, or gunmen, killed and were killed in strikes and disorders, and after the coming of the Republic, which they condemned as just another oppressive capitalistic regime, Anarchist strikes and raids on police barracks kept the countryside in constant turmoil. Peasants flocked to join the CNT, the Anarchist union whose greatest strength was in the oppressed villages of Andalusia, and in the Catalan capital, Barcelona, whose population was swelled by immigrants from the south. The most militant Anarchists were found in the semisecret FAI, whose job was to keep the CNT faithful to the revolution and to serve as its shock troops.

The CNT numbered nearly a million members and vied for supporters with the slightly larger Socialist General Workers Union, the UGT, which was strongest in the mines and factories of north and central Spain. The UGT was an arm of the Socialist Party and, as such, worked for a democratic-socialistic society in which the working class would come to power through legal means. Like other Socialist parties in Europe, it was reformist and cooperated with the liberal middle class. Two Socialist leaders, Indalecio Prieto and Francisco Largo Caballero, were key members of Azaña's Cabinet and the Socialists were the largest single party in the Cortes. Faced with growing support for its Anarchist rival, the CNT, the UGT stepped up efforts to enroll farm workers and, in the process, became more radical. When the CNT wasn't declaring a strike, the UGT was, and when the left-wing unions weren't involved in violence against the rich, they were busy carrying on warfare among themselves. With the working classes in constant turmoil and violence spreading, the keeper of law and order, the army, was growing restive.

The army, which considered itself the protector of Spain's honor, thought that honor was being violated by Azaña's policies. It resented any weakening of the structures of authority, so it disliked the assault on the Church, the growing radicalism of the workers, and, above all, the lessening control of the central government over the provinces, symbolized by Catalan self-government. As guardian of public order, the army traditionally intervened when it felt the government was too weak. The past hundred years had been pockmarked with military revolts and *pronunciamientos*—more than a hundred of them. Since the last military take-over, Primo's coup in 1923, the army had lost its taste for politics. But Azaña knew this might only be a temporary phase and moved to make the army a more loyal and efficient body.

Although strong enough to be the arbiter of national politics, the Spanish army was a weak, comic-opera force—inefficient, with outdated weapons, bribe-ridden, and led by an officer corps whose numbers were swollen far out of proportion to need. It had one officer for every eight men, more majors and captains than sergeants, and 195 generals strutting about in fancy uniforms, helping the military to consume almost a third of the nation's budget.

Azaña went about the business of reorganizing this corpulent body with his usual mixture of sound policies and rash words. He cut the officer corps by two-thirds, persuading surplus officers, especially those with Monarchist sympathies, to retire by generously offering them pensions at full salary. Half the generals were forced to retire, and Azaña concentrated on promoting officers he thought would be loyal to the Republic. He also cut the length of military service, strengthened the neglected air force and the army's noncommissioned officers (corporals and sergeants), and cut the number of military academies. The result was an army that was still far from a modern fighting force but was less of a burden on the nation.

The army accepted these reforms, but officers were furious when Azaña accompanied them with public statements that he would "grind the army down to fine powder" or when he called it "inefficient, vulgar, and pretentious." Some of the retired officers immediately used their new-found leisure to conspire against the government. The distant rumblings of unhappy soldiers and conspirators broke loose in August 1932 when General Sanjurjo led a revolt. It was a sloppy affair, easily put down, and Sanjurjo was sentenced to life imprisonment. The ease with which the rebellion was crushed lulled the government into a sense of false security that was hardly justified by the array of forces opposed to it and by the conspiracies that continued to swirl among the disaffected factions of Spain's former ruling class.

Throughout 1933 the government lost popularity. The "pretty girl" was showing her warts, and the high hopes that had greeted the Republic in the spring of 1931 were turning sour. Its achievements were impressive: it had begun some land reform, increased wages, given self-government to Catalonia, established religious freedom, built a record number of new schools, expanded public works programs, and re-formed the military. But in the process it had outraged the army, embittered the Catholics, frightened the middle class, and disappointed the masses of poor people who were its natural supporters by not moving fast enough or far enough to give them land and food. Strikes and demonstrations were common, and the prisons were full of Anarchists arrested in the almost continuous confrontations between the peasants and the government. The coalition parties were squabbling among themselves, and popular confidence in the government was ebbing.

Faced with a shift in national sentiment, President Alcalá Zamora decided it was time for new elections. The first phase of Spain's experiment in democracy had ended and a new one was about to begin.

# 2

# *The Gathering Storm*

The bitterly contested election campaign laid bare the deep divisions in Spain's society. The Two Spains waged a war without guns: a war for the votes of the Spanish electorate, a war to decide the future of the Republic.

The governing coalition of Left Republicans and Socialists split. Led by Largo Caballero, a veteran union leader and Azaña's Minister of Labor, the Socialists were veering sharply leftward. Their policy of working with the moderate Republicans had failed. Instead of the revolutionary land reforms the Socialists wanted, the government carried out only mild reforms that pushed the peasants and workers into the waiting arms of the more militant Anarchists. So the Socialists decided to campaign independently, believing they could win a majority of the new Cortes.

The Right, however, went into the elections with a united front, led by a new Catholic party, the CEDA, itself a confederation of right-wing Catholic political groups. The CEDA found popular support among Catholics who resented the attacks on the Church's power, and its campaign treasury was swelled by contributions from its allies among the diehard monarchists and rich landowners. José María Gil Robles, who was head of the CEDA, was suspected of Fascist leanings and of disloyalty to the idea of the Republic. His fiery speeches further alarmed his opponents. "We must move toward a new state," he declared in one election address. "What matters if it means shedding blood? . . . Democracy is for us not an end, but a means to go to the conquest of a new state. When the moment comes, either the Cortes will submit or we shall sweep it away."

Among the more than 7 million people who went to the polls on November 19, 1933, were many women voting under the new constitution that erased the men-only tradition in Spanish elections. Most were poorly educated and, far more than their husbands and fathers, relied on the advice of their priests, who influenced many to vote for the CEDA. The Anarchists, angry with the government's repression, organized a massive "don't vote" campaign that kept rural peasants away from the polls. The middle class was more afraid of Largo Caballero's calls for a Socialist state than they were of Gil Robles' apparent fascist tendencies. The result: a stunning victory for the Right. Although the popular vote was fairly evenly divided, Spain's peculiar election laws that favored coalitions gave the Right a nearly 2 to 1 margin in the Cortes.

The President, fearing Gil Robles' program and knowing that the Socialists would do anything to prevent him from becoming Prime Minister, turned instead to Alejandro Lerroux to form a new government. Lerroux was a lion gone tame. In his youth he had been an anti-clerical rabble-rouser known as the "Emperor of the Paralelo," Barcelona's slum district. Age and the spoils of office had mellowed him, and he came to power with a reputation as a corrupt political boss. Promising to roll back many of the reforms of the Azaña period, Lerroux formed a government dependent on the CEDA's votes in the Cortes.

Among the deputies to the new Cortes was a slim young man

whose boyish good looks, easy smile, and pleasing personality masked a determination to set Spain on the path of totalitarian dictatorship. He was José Antonio Primo de Rivera, son of the fallen dictator and the founder of the Falange Española, an avowedly Fascist party modeled on Mussolini's. The Falange's program was ultra-nationalist, with vague dreams of empire abroad and iron discipline coupled with social reforms at home. Early in 1934 José Antonio, as he was always called, merged his party with another fascist group, the JONS. Decked out in their uniform of dark blue shirts, the Falangists made up for their lack of numbers with action in the streets, brawling with leftist youth groups. Spanish fascism was still in its infancy, but with militarism and dictatorships rising all over Europe, few could safely ignore it.

More immediately threatening to the frail Republic was the growing strength of the Monarchists and Carlists whose money was fueling the CEDA's political power and who were actively conspiring to restore the monarchy. The Carlists were the modern-day remnants of the losing side in the civil wars of nineteenth-century Spain, deriving their name from that of their candidate for king in 1833, Don Carlos, whose descendants they believed to be the rightful heirs to the throne. They combined strong individualism and loyalty to local traditions and rights with an almost mystical belief in the unity of king, Church, and nation. Hostile to the political and technological changes of the modern world, they held to their outdated faith with an intensity as hard and as uncompromising as the rocky mountains of their native region, Navarre.

Even Gil Robles was too liberal for the old-line Monarchists and their Carlist allies, and the fact that the government was controlled by right-wing forces did not prevent them from planning rebellion. In March 1934 a Monarchist delegation journeyed to Rome where it won money and arms for a rising from Mussolini. Some 6,000 Carlist volunteers, called *Requetés,* trained by extremist army officers and often led by militant priests, drilled among the hills of Navarre with rifles and machine guns.

With these sounds of thunder coming from the extreme Right, the government slowly reversed the gains made under Azaña. Wages were slashed back to 1931 levels. The countryside was torn by strikes that were ruthlessly suppressed by the Guardia Civil, and thousands of peasants were jailed. Land reforms were suspended, and landlords took revenge on their Socialist and Anarchist workers, many of whom were denied jobs. The laws restricting the Church's privileges were not enforced. General Sanjurjo and his fellow rebels were released from jail, and his new residence in neighboring Portugal became a center for conspiratorial activity. Regional autonomy was threatened.

The mounting misery and rampant repression earned the Center-Right government of 1934–35 the nickname *el bienio negro,* "the black two years." The chasm between the Two Spains was widening dangerously, and the Left was in fear for its life. It believed Gil Robles would soon demand power and institute a Fascist dictatorship like that just established in Austria, where Socialist workers were slaughtered. The Spanish Socialists were alarmed, and their leader, Largo Caballero, threatened that "the proletariat will rise and strike violently at its enemies."

Gil Robles did nothing to calm their fears. A deeply thoughtful, complex man, he was more than just the fledgling dictator his enemies made him out to be. But, like Largo, he was often carried away by demagogic outbursts that chilled more moderate people. On October 1, 1934, he made his move: he withdrew his support from the Cabinet and insisted that the CEDA enter a reorganized government. Ignoring the protests from the Left, the president asked Lerroux to form a new Cabinet that included three *cedistas*.

The Socialists considered it a declaration of war against them and launched a general strike to overthrow the government on October 4. Martial law was declared, the army moved in, and the badly organized and poorly led strike collapsed. In Catalonia President Luis Companys proclaimed a "Catalan state within the Federal Spanish Republic" and invited the opposition parties to set up a government in exile in Barcelona. The army put a swift end to this rebellion and arrested Companys.

Only in the northern mining districts of Asturias did the revolt amount to anything, but there it became the most far-reaching workers' rebellion in Spanish history. Under the slogan UHP (Unite, Proletarian Brothers), 30,000 miners bearing rifles, pistols, and dynamite rose under the leadership of revolutionary committees that included all factions of the Left—Socialists, Anarchists, and Communists. Within two days they controlled much of the province and established a revolutionary regime. Determined to prove the superior morality of the proletariat, the committees protected prisoners from mob vengeance, distributed food and medical care equally, even among their enemies, and were reasonably successful in controlling looting and random violence.

Faced with a full-scale revolution, the government called on General Francisco Franco to direct a counter-attack. Not trusting the draftees of the regular army units to fight poor people like themselves, Franco ordered the battle-tested Moorish mercenaries and the Foreign Legion shipped from their bases in Morocco. Outgunned by the invading armies, who were aided by air attacks, the miners were lost. Village after village fell before the troops, and the provincial capital, Oviedo, was captured after three days of bitter house-to-house fighting that left the city in ruins and its famous university destroyed. Over 2,000 rebels were killed and many more wounded in the fighting and the horrible repression that followed. The Moors and the Legion justified their reputation for brutality by going on a rampage of murder, rape, and pillage. Prisoners were tortured, and when the news leaked out in spite of censorship, the government circulated fictional stories of revolutionary atrocities to justify its own savagery.

A mood of hatred and desperation gripped the Left, revolutionaries and moderates alike, because it felt the Right was using the revolt as an excuse to crush the opposition and restore full power to the oligarchy.

Meanwhile, social conditions worsened. Rents rose and wages were cut, sometimes by 50 percent. Peasants who had settled on the land under the Azaña reforms were evicted. Unemployment rose steadily and almost one out of every four workers was without a job. In some places the situation reached such a level of desperation that men were working for a dish of soup and a crust of bread instead of wages.

In the fall of 1935 the government was rocked by scandals involving CEDA's Cabinet partners, Lerroux's Radical Party. The Radicals had played musical chairs with Cabinet seats, shuffling their members in and out of ministries so they would qualify for lifetime pensions as ex-ministers. Then it was revealed that high party officials and relatives of Lerroux took bribes to introduce a new gambling game, *straperlo*, into Spain's resort areas. The word *"straperlo"* soon became a synonym for shady dealings in high places, much as "Watergate" has passed into the current American vocabulary. Finally, in December, stories of corruption involving contracts for army supplies in Morocco helped bring the government down.

With the Radicals disgraced, Gil Robles expected the president to name him Prime Minister. Instead, Alcalá Zamora dissolved the Cortes, appointed a caretaker government headed by Manuel Portela Valladares, and scheduled new elections. Furious at being passed over, Gil Robles considered mounting a coup, but backed off when the cautious General Franco told him he could not support one.

The Left had learned its lessons from the 1933 electoral disaster. All parties, from the extreme Left to the liberal Center and including the small but fast-growing Communist Party, united in a Popular Front behind a single list of candidates and a common program. The Right went into the election divided. Gil Robles' political opportunism during his brief period of power had made the rich landowners who bankrolled him distrustful, and the CEDA entered the election alone in most districts. Even the enthusiastic crowds shouting "All Power to the Chief" could not overcome the party's weakness.

Once again the political pendulum shifted. The Popular Front won a resounding victory in the February 1936 elections. It captured a clear majority of the seats in the Cortes and ran up 4.2 million votes against about 3.8 million for the parties of the Right. The parties of the Center could only muster a mere 680,000 votes, revealing Spain's division into two camps, each unalterably opposed to the other.

Immediately after the election results were known, the Prime Minister was placed under tremendous pressure by General Franco and others to declare martial law and establish a dictatorship with army backing. Franco knew the army was not yet at the point where it would rebel on its own, but it would stand behind a quasi-legal action by the civilian government to overturn the Popular Front victory. The frightened Portela resigned immediately and a new government headed by Azaña was hastily sworn in. Disgusted.

Franco and the army plotters spent the coming months planning the rebellion for which the civilian rightists lacked the courage.

One of the first moves Azaña made upon taking office was to disperse the military plotters. Franco was sent to command the military garrison in the Canary Islands, off the coast of Africa. General Manuel Goded was moved to the Balearic Islands in the Mediterranean. Other known anti-Popular Front officers were shifted to provincial outposts or to potentially less dangerous assignments.

Azaña then started to implement the Popular Front program. The suspended anti-clerical laws were revived and enforced. The political prisoners were set free. Self-government was restored to Catalonia and to the Basque region, as well as to those Socialist towns whose governments had been taken over by the Madrid government after the October 1934 revolt. Rents were suspended in Andalusia and Estremadura, and landlords forced to take back workers fired after the 1934 strikes and to make up their lost wages. A broader agrarian reform program settled 70,000 peasants on their own land in March alone. But there was still no massive land redistribution and no socialization of the powerful banks that controlled the economy. "We want peace and order," Azaña told a French interviewer. "We are moderate."

Too moderate for the working class, which had tasted the fruits of victory after the black two years of reactionary rule and which now was in a revolutionary mood. Events were moving swiftly and the government could no longer control the mass occupation of land by peasants unconcerned with legal details, or the striking workers in the cities whose thrust for power led to a series of conflicts with the police. In May, Azaña became president of the Republic and, probably with a good deal of relief, moved into the presidential palace and turned the government over to his friend Santiago Casares Quiroga.

The Spain inherited by the Casares Cabinet was on the verge of chaos. Political antagonisms had become so deep that deputies toted handguns and were frisked as they entered the Cortes. The countryside was rocked by violence as impatient peasants seized land throughout the south. In the southwestern province of Badajoz, 60,000 peasants crying *Viva la Republica* occupied untilled land. Troops pushed them off, but as soon as the soldiers left the peasants were back. Finally, the government simply declared the seizures legal. In the cities so many industries were hit by strikes that newspapers took to carrying strike box-scores as if they were reporting football results, and the rivalry between the Socialist and Anarchist unions led to frequent gunfights.

The government could hardly be blamed for its failure to control the situation. It was reaping the bitter harvest of the *bienio negro* that had abandoned moderate reforms, drastically worsened the lives of the poor, and encouraged extremism. The election victory of the Popular Front had led to expectations that were so high as to be impossible to fulfill. Even if the government were to settle every landless peasant on his own farm, Spain as a nation was too poor to provide the seed, tools, and credit necessary. If the Republic had come to power in a violent revolution that destroyed the ruling oligarchy, it might have been able to nationalize land, banks, and industry while unifying the working class. But the Republic itself was the fruit of a compromise with the middle class that wanted order, political liberty, and an end to the monarchy, and was relatively less concerned with social and economic equality that would endanger its own status. So the Spanish Republic in that fateful spring of 1936 thrashed blindly in the dark, struggling for a way to survive.

The political situation was deteriorating at an alarming rate. Largo Caballero's followers hailed him as "the Spanish Lenin" and were demanding a "worker's government." Largo hoped the moderate Cabinet would be replaced with a socialist regime that would institute radical reforms. But Indalecio Prieto, Largo's chief rival for party leadership, warned against the continued disorder and cautioned that "what a nation cannot survive is the waste of public power and economic strength in a constant state of uneasiness, of anxiety, and worry."

Extremism mounted on the Right, as well. As Gil Robles' star waned, that of José Calvo Sotelo, a Monarchist with pronounced Fascist leanings, rose. Both men actively conspired with the generals plotting a military rebellion. More people began to turn to José Antonio's Falange as a refuge against leftist revolution and the government's policy of appeasing the Left. Falange gunmen roamed the streets, conducted lightning terror raids into Socialist neighborhoods, and kept the seething caldron of violence overflowing.

In April the CEDA youth organization merged with the Falange, whose violence escalated with the coming of milder weather. A judge who sentenced a Falangist for the murder of a Socialist newsboy was himself assassinated. An attempt was made on Azaña's life. Each outrage by the Falange had its counterpart in a reprisal action by the Left, and the extremists of both sides conducted an active, undeclared war in the streets of Spain's cities. In the first six months after the election, the police listed some 215 people killed and more than 500 wounded in political violence, and the real toll is believed to have been much higher.

The government outlawed the Falange and jailed José Antonio and other top leaders of the party, but the rank-and-file members increased their violence. The macabre dance of death reached a crescendo on July 12, 1936, when Falangists gunned down Lieutenant José Castillo, an officer of the Assault Guards who had killed a party member at a riot some months earlier.

When word of Castillo's murder reached his friends, they decided on swift retribution. That night, a group of Assault Guards, in uniform and driving official marked police cars, set out to murder a prominent rightist. They went to Calvo Sotelo's home, told him they had orders for his arrest, and asked him to come to the police station. When he tried to call police headquarters to confirm this, he found the wires cut. Although his family implored him not to go, he decided to join the Guards after their captain promised he would be safely at police headquarters in five minutes. Calvo Sotelo told his wife he would call her from there, "unless these gentlemen have come to blow out my brains." And that, in a police van rolling along the silent night streets of the city, is exactly what they did.

The murders of Castillo and Calvo Sotelo set the final seal on the division of Spain into two unreconcilable factions. The two men were buried in the same graveyard on the same day, and with them, Spain's hopes for some kind of peaceful settlement. The large crowds of mourners that attended their funerals exchanged glares of hate across the protective police barriers that separated the hostile groups. The scene at the cemetery was symbolic—half of Spain could no longer live with the other half. The glue that had held Spain together for the past five stormy years had come unstuck, and the Republic, born to such high hopes in 1931, now awaited the inevitable war that would seal its fate.

# 3

# *Rebellion*

The military rebellion that would sweep democratic government in Spain into oblivion came after long months of planning and tortuous negotiations among the forces on the Right.

Its leader was General Emilio Mola Vidal, the commander of the Pamplona military district, stronghold of the Carlists. Mola, who came from a long line of military men, had been commander of the army in Morocco and later was security chief for the monarchy. He wove a net of conspiracy that brought together the disparate elements of Spain's right-wing opposition. Within the army, Mola worked with a semisecret officers organization, the UME, that honeycombed the officer corps with anti-Popular Front agitators in every garrison. The plot was bankrolled by the CEDA and by Calvo Sotelo's Monarchists. Mola expected help from the Falange and from the Carlists. General Sanjurjo, exiled in Portugal, lent his name to the operation and was expected to take over in Madrid after the success of the rebellion.

Mola planned a swift, brutal rising that would crush the Left once and for all. "The action must be violent in the extreme," he ordered, "in order to crush the enemy, who is strong and well organized, as soon as possible. All leaders of political parties, associations, or trade unions not joining the movement will be arrested and exemplary punishments meted out to strangle strikes and rebellions."

As spring crept into summer, Mola almost despaired of getting the rebellion off the ground. The government broke up several other army plots. The Carlists were stubbornly demanding guarantees that the future state would be anti-democratic and monarchist, and that they would rule supreme in Navarre. José Antonio, from his prison cell, was chafing at the bit, impatiently urging Mola to action and insisting that the Falange's program be the model for the future Spain. Mola desperately tried to juggle these warring factions, all the while fearing that the government would find out about the plot. His biggest worry was the cool response of so many generals to his plans; unable to unite the army's generals or to drum up the required enthusiasm, he postponed the scheduled date for the rising several times. The cagey Mola had no intention of sticking his neck out in an old-fashioned *pronunciamiento,* for he realized his rebellion would "cost much blood and many tears."

Franco was a big problem, too. Before going off to the Canary Islands, he conferred with a group of generals and all agreed to keep in touch. The best known, most popular, and most efficient of all Spain's generals, his cooperation was essential to success. Franco had had a meteoric rise through the ranks, always the youngest major, the youngest colonel, and then the youngest general in the army. His reputation had been earned in the parched deserts of Morocco where he commanded the brutal Foreign Legion. Despite his small size, he inspired fear in these most hardened of men. "He simply looks blankly at a fellow, with very big and very serious eyes, and says, 'Execute him' and walks away, just like that," a veteran of Franco's Legion said. "I've seen murderers go white in the face because Franco had looked at them out of the corner of his eye. You know, that man's not quite human and he hasn't got any nerves." He was loved as well as hated by the hardened legionnaires, and his courage and luck under fire made him venerated by the common soldiers and by the Moorish mercenaries, who believed he led a charmed life.

A dashing battlefield figure, Franco was super-cautious in other matters, especially political ones. He refused to save Gil Robles when the CEDA leader asked his help in 1935, and he agreed to back a coup in February 1936 only if the Portela government would provide a legal cover for army action. Now, he kept himself open to the plots but refused to take full part in them until he was sure they would be successful. His slow, cautious attitude drove the conspirators to the edge of frenzy. Sanjurjo told his followers, "With or without Franky-boy, we shall save Spain," and José Antonio labeled him "the biggest chicken of all." It was partly to get Franco to commit himself that Mola issued a warning that "he who is not with us is against us, and will be treated as an enemy."

Sometime around the beginning of July 1936 Franco finally came around. But he exacted a high price. He was to take command of the Army of Africa in the rebellion. This was the elite force, which Franco had helped build during his days in the Legion. If the little general was going to take risks, it would be at the head of the best fighters in the Spanish army.

With Franco finally aboard, the pieces of the plot started falling swiftly into place. On July 12 a compromise was reached with the Carlists, and in the following days instructions were given to friendly officers in units throughout Spain and the Moroccan Protectorate. When news of Calvo Sotelo's assassination came to Mola's headquarters, all was in readiness. In Madrid Socialist leaders implored Casares Quiroga to distribute arms to forestall a military take-over, but the Prime Minister dismissed both the proposal to turn guns over to potential revolutionaries and the idea that the army might revolt.

It started in Melilla, a sleepy town on the Mediterranean coast of Spanish Morocco. Rebel officers seized main buildings and the radio station and crushed resistance in the workers' quarters. Within hours grim-faced troops were hunting down known leftists and arresting those they did not shoot on the spot. As Prime Minister Casares Quiroga was telephoning the High Commissioner to resist, legionnaires were crushing opposition in Tetuán and Ceuta, the other main towns in Morocco. By evening on the 17th, Colonel Juan Yagüe was sending telegrams to mainland garrisons informing them that the rising was a success.

In the Canaries, Franco proclaimed a state of war, and his troops repeated the terror tactics of the Moroccan garrisons. Early on July 18 he went on the radio with a manifesto explaining that the rising was to save Spain from destruction by anarchy, Russian agents, "revolutionary hordes," and separatists.

Then he boarded the *Dragon Rapide*, a private plane rented from an English company by Monarchist plotters, and headed for Morocco to take command of the Army of Africa. On Sunday, July 19, his craft glided over the sun-brightened minarets of Tetuán and circled low over the airfield as Franco tensely studied the faces of officers below trying to recognize friends. Spotting Colonel Eduardo Sáenz de Buruaga, he ordered the plane to land and stepped onto the hot pavement of the field to be greeted by a smiling Sáenz, whose first words were *"sin novedad"* ("nothing new"), the secret password of the rebels, whose real meaning was "all is well."

At that very moment, in Madrid, power was passing from

the established government to the trade unions and workers'
groups. The official radio broadcast optimistic news reports
that everything was under control and that the minor *pronunciamiento* of Franco's would be crushed. But few believed
the official line, and the Puerta del Sol was mobbed by thousands of Madrileños demanding that the government distribute
arms to the people. Both factions of the Socialists united in
the quest for guns, and banner headlines screamed "ARMS,
ARMS, ARMS," from every newsstand. Casares Quiroga, refusing to preside over the dismantling of a moderate state,
rejected these demands. Finally, with the streets of Madrid
in the hands of armed patrols of Socialist militants and with
reports pouring in from the provinces of more rebellious
garrisons, he resigned on the night of July 18.

His successor, Diego Martínez Barrio, held office for only
a few hours, just long enough to fail in his efforts to reach a
compromise with the military. He called Mola early on July
19, while Franco was settling into his new office in Morocco,
and proposed the formation of a "national unity government" including all political factions except for the extreme
Left, with Mola as Minister of War. "It is too late, it is too
late," Mola replied. "If you and I were to reach a compromise
we should betray our ideals as well as our followers. We
would both deserve to be lynched." The failure of the attempted compromise, coupled with the fact that junior
officers were already unloading arms-laden trucks at Socialist headquarters in defiance of the orders of a now powerless
government, led Martínez to resign.

Azaña next turned to José Giral, a chemistry professor and
political moderate, who bowed to the inevitable: he distributed
guns and munitions to the workers' organizations and called
on Spain to resist. "When I took charge," Giral later wrote,
"I had to consider that the only way of combating the mili-

tary rising was to hand the people the few arms we had at our disposal." The optimistic messages broadcast by Madrid radio gave way to calls for mass resistance. Dolores Ibarruri, better known by the affectionate nickname "La Pasionaria," took to the air with the slogan, "It is better to die on your feet than live on your knees!" All Spain took up her cry of *"No Paserán"* ("They Shall Not Pass"). Popular enthusiasm now reached new heights. Spaniards on both sides had been spoiling for a fight to the finish. Now it was at hand: no compromises, no quarter given. The Two Spains hurled themselves against each other furiously that bloody weekend.

While the government floundered in indecision, attempting compromise and hoping the outbreak could be confined to Morocco, the rebels were capturing key provinces. Seville, the biggest city in the south, was the first to fall, taken almost single-handedly by General Gonzalo Queipo de Llano on Saturday, July 18, one day after the rising began in Morocco. Accompanied only by two other officers, Queipo marched into the army garrison, arrested the loyal commander, and, meeting no resistance at all, placed other officers under arrest until he found one willing to lead the troops under his orders. "From time to time," he wrote, "I had to rub my eyes to make sure I was not dreaming." His bluff successful, Queipo marched his handful of rebel troops into a brief skirmish with Assault Guards, then occupied the city. Loyal officials and officers were shot, police files of known leftists were used as aids in hunting down hundreds who were arrested and shot, and an attempted general strike was broken by machine guns. By nightfall the center of Seville was in the rebels' grip. After Moorish reinforcements arrived on the 20th, the outlying workers' districts fell and their residents were slaughtered.

Elsewhere in the south the rebels had mixed success. They captured the port of Cádiz, which became the jumping-off point for troops from Africa, and they took Córdoba and Granada, brutally overcoming the resistance of unarmed protesters. Everywhere that weekend people were clamoring for weapons with which to fight the rebels, but local officials refused to distribute arms without direct orders from Madrid, where the government delayed arming the people for fear of social revolution. This delay led to the loss of many cities to the army, and almost led to the loss of others, such as Valencia and Alicante.

The rebels were often hampered by the refusal of senior officers to join them, or by the indecision of some who did. Many generals who thoroughly disliked the Popular Front government held off joining the rebellion for fear that its failure would mean death or imprisonment. Málaga was saved for the Republic by the hesitations of its military commander, who occupied the center of town and then marched his troops back to their barracks and listened to telephoned pleas from the Madrid government to give them time to work out a compromise. By the next day, July 19, workers and loyal Assault Guards had surrounded the troops and forced their surrender.

In the north the rebels were easily successful in traditionally conservative areas where they had the support of the population. Mola declared a state of war from Pamplona's town square, where he was greeted by the *"vivas"* of the Carlists waving their brilliant red and yellow Monarchist flags and singing old songs from their wars of the nineteenth century. In other sections, where the people were loyal to the government or where there was a strong leftist movement, battles raged, often ferocious ones. Where the rebels won, it was because of their superior arms, the desertion to their side by police and Assault Guards, or because they acted too swiftly for their opponents to organize. Oviedo, the capital of radical Asturias, was won by trickery. Its commander, Colonel Antonio Aranda, pretended to be loyal to the government and helped send a trainload of miners to defend Madrid. Once they were out of the way, he telephoned ahead to have their train captured and took over the city himself. The pattern following a rebel victory was always the same: troops and armed bands of Falangists arrested all known leftists and Republicans, and marauders burned local union headquarters and conducted terror raids to cow the population.

As the long weekend wore on, the pattern of victories and defeats showed that the arming of the people was the main element in keeping the Republic alive. Nowhere was this seen more clearly than in Madrid and Barcelona, the two largest and most important cities in the country. In Madrid the conspirators hesitated because of the hostility of the population, which, by the afternoon of July 18, possessed some guns. Rebel General Joaquín Fanjul holed up in the Montaña Barracks, a fortress overlooking the center of the city. It wasn't until the next evening that he decided to march his troops out, but by then the barracks were surrounded by union militiamen, loyal Assault Guards, and thousands of civilians milling about in a carnival atmosphere. On the 20th the white flag of surrender appeared at a window. Three times the flag was shown; three times the advancing crowd was machine-gunned. When the crowd, maddened by this betrayal, which may have been the result of confusion within the barracks, overpowered the garrison, it killed dozens of officers.

In Barcelona mobs thronged the central avenue, the Ramblas, throughout the night of July 18–19, exhorted by an array of loudspeakers to defend the Republic. At dawn officers marched troops from their barracks in defiance of the loyal commanding general. Bands of armed workers, loyal troops, and Assault Guards, and—almost unique in Spain that weekend—loyal Guardias, met them in pitched battles that covered the city with the smell of blood and death. Rebel cannon, mounted at key intersections, fired down the long avenues and ripped holes in buildings that held resisters. Workers were fired on from church steeples, and the popping sounds of machine-gun fire filled the air. Heavy fighting dislodged rebel machine-gun nests from the city center and hundreds of dead and wounded lay sprawled in the Plaza de Cataluña, the main square. In some places truly remarkable scenes occurred as unarmed workers rushed up to rebel fortifications and begged the soldiers not to fire on their own people and not to rise against the Republic that had promised so much to poor people like themselves. The troops, who had been told they were there to put down an Anarchist revolt, dropped their weapons or turned them on their own officers.

By nightfall the city was shrouded in smoke from destroyed buildings and burning churches. Except for some pockets of resistance the rebellion was crushed. General Manuel Goded, who had flown in from the Balearics to take command, was captured and broadcast an appeal to his followers to surrender.

By July 21 the Two Spains assumed a recognizable shape after the confusion of the weekend's fighting. The rebels were in control of Morocco and the Balearic Islands and held a wide band of mainland Spain from the French border on the east to the Portuguese border and the Atlantic Ocean on the west. They also maintained strongholds around a few large southern cities, such as Seville and Córdoba, and a half-moon shaped area in Cádiz that gave them control of the Strait of Gibraltar. The Republic retained most of south and central Spain, the Levant and Catalonia in the east, and a broad strip of northern provinces, including the Basque region, on the Bay of Biscay.

The rebels were separated, with Franco's army stranded in Morocco and Mola's forces confined to the north. They also lost their titular leader, General José Sanjurjo, when the small plane taking him from Portugal to rebel headquarters in Burgos was overburdened by the weight of his uniform-crammed suitcases and crashed during takeoff.

It is impossible to determine the exact strength of the armies of the Two Spains that chaotic mid-July. The Republic could not count on the remnants of the regular army in its territory since many of its officers were loyal to geography—finding themselves in the Loyalist zone, they hid their rebel sympathies and pretended to support the Republic. The rebels had roughly 30,000 soldiers on the Spanish mainland, including Guardias, as well as another 12,000 well-trained Carlist militia and about 20,000 Falangists. The Republic's 10,000 soldiers and Assault Guards were beefed up by tens of thousands of party and trade-union militiamen. The most powerful force on either side, the 30,000 superb fighters of the Army of Africa, were entirely with the rebels. The problem was how to get them from Morocco to Spain.

The conspirators expected the navy to ferry these troops to the Spanish mainland, but on most ships sailors mutinied, killed their officers, and blockaded the Moroccan coast. Franco tried to send some of his soldiers across the Strait in small boats and planes, and even strapped Moorish troops to the wings of some of the airplanes to increase capacity, but it was obvious that he would need a fleet of transport planes to do the job.

Aided by German businessmen in Morocco, including some

leaders of the local Nazi Party, approaches were made to
Hitler for help. Another delegation flew from Franco's headquarters to Rome to ask Mussolini for a dozen airplanes that,
Franco promised, would help him win the war in a few days.
Mola sent agents of his own to get aid from the two dictators,
resulting in considerable confusion until the Germans and
Italians realized the generals were both on the same side.
Franco, better known and in command of the better army, was
the man both powers looked to as chief of the rebels, although Mola had originated the plot and now presided over
a junta of top officers that did not yet include Franco.

On July 28 the first German planes, twenty Junker heavy
transports, arrived in Tetuán and their German crews began
the regular routine of ferrying rebel troops to Seville four
times a day. The Italians also sent aircraft, a dozen bombers,
three of which ran out of fuel over French Morocco and
landed there, exposing the secret operation to the world's
scrutiny. When Republican vessels brought their anti-aircraft
guns into action, the Germans and Italians bombed them out
of the water. The end of the Republican blockade came on
August 5, when 3,000 men were shipped across the Strait
in a small fleet of vessels protected by aircraft. A jubilant
Franco wired Mola, "We are masters of the Strait; we are in
command of the situation," and flew 600,000 rounds of
ammunition to the northern army. On August 6 Franco installed himself in a palace in Seville to direct the Army of
Africa's march to Madrid, and in the days that followed,
German and Italian men and equipment continued to flow into
rebel territory.

Meanwhile, the Republic frantically sought aid from other
countries. As the legal government threatened by an unlaw-
ful military rebellion, it was entitled to such aid under international law. The Giral government turned first to neigh-

boring France, which was also governed by a Popular Front coalition and whose premier, Léon Blum, was a Socialist friendly to the Spanish Republic. Because of the power of the right-wing opposition in French politics and Britain's insistence on strict neutrality, Blum could not openly help the Republic, but he did send about fifty outdated aircraft and allowed volunteers and paid technicians to flow across the open border.

The German and Italian aid turned the tide for the rebel forces. Throughout the summer, they transported 25,000 Army of Africa troops to Spain, including new recruits raised with the help of local Arab chieftains. The arms and munitions they brought Mola saved the Army of the North. After the widespread failures of the first weekend of revolt, Mola was dejected. He had to abandon his original plan of concentrating all his forces on a march to Madrid because the loss of the northern provinces to the Republic left his flanks exposed. Instead, about 5,000 soldiers and Carlist *Requetés* moved into the mountains above the capital, where they met an advancing Republican militia. Urgently asked for ammunition, Mola had to wire the rebel commander of that army: "Impossible to send ammunition. I have 26,000 cartridges for all the Army of the North." His secretary later wrote that by July 29 the general was thinking of suicide. Then came Franco's wire, followed by all the ammunition he could use, but by that time the loyal militia occupied the heights above Madrid and the Republic's capital was safe.

Both sides dug in for what they knew would be a long, hard-fought war. The rebels called themselves Nationalists, and labeled their cause The Movement, or The Crusade. The Republicans were known as the Loyalists. Although the Republic had staved off disaster, held a temporary superiority in arms, and had caught the imagination of most of the world's liberal forces, it faced a grim future against a tenacious enemy lavishly aided by two powerful dictatorships. Locked in this life-and-death struggle, the Republic now embarked on a thoroughgoing social revolution the likes of which had never been seen in Spain's long history.

# *4*

# *Revolution*

The military revolt was the push that sent Spain's tottering political structure crumbling to the ground. The government was plunged into chaos, and the power that lay in the streets was picked up by armed militants of trade unions and radical factions.

During the weekend of July 17–19 many of the people who ran the country—the soldiers, the bureaucrats, the postmen and telegraph operators, the diplomats and the police—had either gone over to the rebel side or were trapped in the third of Spain controlled by them.

Loyal Spain was now effectively ruled not by government officials but by workmen's committees, trade unions, and left-wing party militias. "The government would do absolutely nothing," wrote Juan Negrín, who later became Prime Minister, "because neither our frontiers nor our ports were in its hands. They were in the hands of individuals, of local, district, or provincial bodies, and naturally the government could not make its authority felt." The army claimed to be saving Spain from anarchy and revolution; instead, it pushed the country over the brink into a revolutionary situation. In Madrid the Socialist union, the UGT, ran public services and controlled the food supply. In Catalonia real power was wielded by the Anarchist-dominated Anti-Fascist Militias Committee. Towns and villages throughout the country were run by the political parties strongest in that region. When the American ambassador, Claude Bowers, wanted to drive into the Basque country to observe the situation firsthand, he needed permits from five separate political groups.

"The people are no longer fighting for the Spain of July 16, which was still a Spain socially dominated by the traditional castes, but for a Spain from which those castes are definitely eliminated," declared the Socialist newspaper *Claridad*. "The most powerful support for the war lies in the total uprooting of fascism, economically and in every other way. That is revolution."

Terror is the handmaiden of social revolution, and both sectors of warring Spain were plunged into terrorist campaigns to eliminate their enemies. In Loyalist Spain the summer of 1936 was the time of the "red terror" to destroy the power of the traditional ruling classes. It was a spontaneous movement, born of the long pent-up hatreds of Spanish workers for those who had exploited them.

Nearly everywhere murder squads set forth to eliminate rebel sympathizers whose class positions—businessmen, landowners, priests—marked them as potential enemies of the revolution. As always in Spain, the special target of revolutionaries was the Church. All over the countryside churches went up in flames and priests were shot. "D'you know who's our main enemy?" a peasant asked Franz Borkenau, a sociologist visiting a Catalan village. "The priests and the monks. Then come the generals and the officers. And after that, of course, the rich."

Excepting the devout Basque provinces, churches in the Republic were closed down and priests traded their robes for civilian clothes to ensure their safety. More than 7,000 priests, nuns, monks, and church functionaries were murdered in the terror. A number of priests were helped to escape by authorities unable to control the terrorists. Some clerics later acknowledged that their actions had helped cause the terrible vengeance of the people. "The Reds have destroyed our churches, but we first destroyed the Church," admitted one priest who fled to France.

Some of the terror reflected blind violence, a lashing out against members of another class, but often the targets were selected because of their past actions. Priests who hurried through the funeral of a poor man while lavishing attention on the rich, doctors who ignored poor patients, and lawyers who served the large landowners were all doomed. In general, though, it was sufficient for a person to own property, to be a member of a right-wing party, or just to be thought hostile to the revolution for him to be in danger.

In the larger cities the terror was organized by revolutionary committees that compared lists of prospective victims; names that appeared on all the lists were doomed. Justice was dispensed by kangaroo courts that hauled people before them on the word of informers, sometimes individuals out to settle private grudges. Victims were "taken for a ride"— driven to the outskirts of town, then shot. The gunmen were often simple criminals masquerading as revolutionaries, or gangs of teen-agers drunk with violence.

After the first terrible weeks of killing, a reaction set in and attempts were made to stop the terror. The Anarchists of the CNT and the FAI threatened to kill such free-wheeling assassins. "Smash the riff-raff," the FAI ordered. "If we do not, the crooks will smash the revolution by dishonoring it." The government radio constantly broadcast warnings to people to lock their doors, to refuse to admit any militiamen to their buildings, and to call the police if presumed killer

squads were in their neighborhoods. It also helped nearly
20,000 people, including prominent right-wingers, to take
refuge in foreign embassies and assisted those embassies to
rent nearby buildings in which to house them.

This was in strong contrast to the parallel terror in the
Nationalist zone, a terror encouraged and ordered by the
government there, a terror that did not allow political asylum
and that was carried out in large part by the forces of law
and order—the police and the army. The "red terror" lasted
throughout the summer and reached its climax in late August,
when rumors of a prison riot and news of the mass slaughter
of civilians in Badajoz by the rebels led to the massacre of
seventy political prisoners in Madrid. After that, the government slowly restored a measure of control. The *paseos*, or
"death rides," became less frequent and a semblance of
order was maintained.

The terror, like previous outbursts in other countries and in
other eras, accompanied a far-reaching social revolution.
Everywhere, workers were in power. "It was the first time
that I had ever been in a town where the working class was
in the saddle," wrote George Orwell, who arrived in Barcelona in late 1936. "Practically every building of any size
had been seized by the workers and was draped with red
flags or with the red and black flag of the Anarchists; every
wall was scrawled with the hammer and sickle and with the
initials of the revolutionary parties." Along the brightly lit
Ramblas, revolutionary songs bellowed from loudspeakers
and no neckties or hats were to be seen, only the blue over-
alls of the militiamen or the open shirts of workmen. Signs in
barber shops explained that barbers were no longer slaves;
every shop had a sign proclaiming that it was "collectivized,"
and waiters replaced "sir" with "comrade" in cafés and

restaurants. "Above all," Orwell wrote, "there was a belief in the revolution and the future, a feeling of having suddenly emerged into an era of equality and freedom."

Orwell may have romanticized his account somewhat, but there was no mistaking the popular enthusiasm for the revolution or the fervor with which people threw themselves into the building of a new society. Neighborhood committees made up of Popular Front representatives took control of buildings and utilities; hotels and right-wing party headquarters were taken over by leftist groups for their headquarters or were turned into orphanages; and shops and factories were taken over by their workers. Sometimes such collectivization simply meant that the workers now shared in the profits; at other times it meant direct control by union committees, with the owner, if he had escaped the terror and did not flee, now working alongside his former employees. Often, unsafe factories were closed down, their machinery moved to a new building, and the business reopened under the workers' control. It has been estimated that a third of Madrid's businesses, half of Valencia's, and two-thirds of Barcelona's were collectivized under some form of worker control or participation.

The real revolution however, took place in the countryside. More than one thousand agricultural collectives sprang into being in the wake of the rebellion. Nearly three hundred of these were in Aragon and are said to have included over 200,000 people. The collectives were run by elected committees responsible to the community, and they governed nearly every aspect of village life, a throwback to the assemblies of all adult males that had governed communities in Spain's medieval period. Often committee memberships were rotated among all citizens to prevent abuses of power. Conditions

varied widely, but nearly everywhere property records were
burned and land was either pooled and run collectively by
committee or broken up into plots for each family.

In some of the collectives run by Anarchists all money was
abolished. One newspaper crowed: "Rockefeller, if you
were to come to Fraga [a village in Aragon] with your entire
bank account you would not be able to buy a cup of coffee.
Money, your God and your servant, has been abolished here
and the people are happy." In some places, like Fraga, money
was replaced by committee-issued vouchers exchangeable
for food or goods in the communal dining hall or in the shops.
Generally, the value of the vouchers was related to a person's
need, that is, to the size of his family or other special require-
ments, rather than to the value of the work he did. Some
villages were puritanical, banning liquor, coffee, and tobacco.
The goal was to create a humane, moral life rather than to
enjoy the luxuries of the village's former rulers.

In Calanda, another Anarchist village, an observer wrote:
"What was once the church is now a food warehouse. The new
meat market is in the annex, hygienic and elegant, such as
the village has never known. No purchases are made with
money. The women receive meat in exchange for coupons without paying anything or rendering any service. They belong
to the collective and that is sufficient to entitle them to food."
In some places collectivization was imposed on everyone; in
others it was a matter of choice and people were allowed to
till their own farms or run their own businesses. In still other
villages, everything was as before, except for the replace-
ment of landlords by the committee; workers continued on
their old jobs at their old salaries and the "revolution" seemed
a long way off.

The record of this rural revolution that swept Spain in the
summer of 1936 is mixed; in some places it was a great suc-

cess, in others, a failure. The lack of coordination among the many independent villages made it difficult for the wartime government to plan its food production or distribute food efficiently, and the basic poverty of the countryside remained intact. But, for the first time, the beaten bottom layer of Spain's population felt itself in control of its own destiny. The poorest of Spain's villages, once scenes of unrelieved misery, were still poor, but they were now infused with a sense of social justice and equality that inspired the peasants and gave them new hope. Such an accomplishment defies measurement by the ordinary yardsticks of production figures and net income.

A measure of the popular support for the Republic was the enthusiasm with which people joined militia units to fight the rebels. With the bulk of the army in revolt, the government's main line of defense was the hastily gathered militia units fielded by political parties and trade unions. This was a raggle-taggle army that made up in high morale what it lacked in spit and polish. Wearing improvised uniforms and party badges or union insignias stuck in their caps, these "soldiers" ranged in age from boys in their teens to men in their fifties, and sometimes included women. Discipline was nonexistent, and the only preparation many got before marching off to the front lines was some half-hearted close-order drill or some political sloganeering.

Their lack of realism was sometimes pathetic. Catalonian Anarchists marched off to the Aragon front without the shovels they needed to dig trenches. "We are going to the front to fight and die," they said, "not to work." They often named themselves after revolutionary heroes and events, or for the power they presumed to wield: thirty-three companies took the name "Steel."

The government knew that such a force could not stand up

to Franco's powerful army, then making its way toward Madrid from the south. Proposals to rebuild the regular army were rebuffed. "We will go to the militia. To the front as well," declared an Anarchist newspaper. "But to go to the barracks as before, soldiers subject to discipline and orders which do not come from the popular forces, No." They feared that a new government-controlled army would stop the revolution in its tracks.

Oddly enough, the loudest voices calling for government control of the militias were the Communists, whose own militia unit, the Fifth Regiment, was the most powerful force on the Madrid front, almost alone among the militia units in its discipline and training. Half of its members were non-Communists when they joined; they were attracted to the unit because of the skill of its commanders and the seriousness with which it went about the business of organizing for war. By the end of 1936 the Fifth Regiment numbered 60,000 troops, and the Communist Party supplied it with officers and political advisers.

The Communists were hardheaded realists and understood that Franco's professional soldiers could only be beaten by a disciplined Republican army under the unified command of a centralized government. They joined with the moderate Republican government in defending small businessmen and farmers and condemned forced collectivization of private property. They were willing to temporarily forgo the achievement of a Communist system in favor of moderate policies that would unify the country against the common danger and allay the fears of potential allies, such as France and England, who might be frightened away by a "red" revolution.

By summer's end, public opinion was split between those who wanted to halt the social revolution in order to give complete national attention to the struggle against the rebellion

and those who wanted a two-front war—a military fight
against the enemy and a social revolution in the fields and
factories. Just about everyone agreed, though, that the weak
Republican government of Giral had to be replaced by one
that more adequately reflected the balance of political forces
in the country. The war was going badly: a Republican attempt to capture the Balearic Islands failed, the rebels made
gains in the north, an attempt to capture Córdoba resulted in
a Loyalist defeat, and Franco's army was marching relentlessly toward the capital from the south.

Azaña swallowed his distaste for Largo Caballero and on
September 4 named him Prime Minister of what was called
the "Government of Victory." The new government was a
coalition of left-wing Popular Front parties, with six Socialists, including Largo's party rival, Indalecio Prieto, four
Republicans, a Catalan and a Basque, and two Communists,
marking the first time in history that Communists joined a
coalition government—one, moreover, that included a prominent Catholic layman. The Anarchists refused to join the
government, but promised it their support.

Largo Caballero, after years of talking revolution and
drinking the heady wine of being acclaimed the "Spanish
Lenin," now set out to govern the country. He was torn by his
deep sympathy for the social revolution and the militia system and by the realization that both had to be brought under
control to centralize the war effort. His enthusiasm for communist theory did not extend to the practices of the Spanish
Communist Party, and he wanted to limit its growing influence without damaging relations with Russia, from whom
he hoped to get military aid.

As Premier and Minister of War, Largo Caballero quickly
forgot about the revolutionary program of nationalization and
revolution he had pressed since 1934 and turned first to re-

building the shattered central government. The power that had fragmented like so many pieces of broken glass had to be reassembled by a strong government in Madrid if the Republic was to survive. One of Giral's last acts was an order to replace the Guardia Civil, or what was left of it in the Republican zone, with a new body, the National Republican Guard. Largo Caballero encouraged recruitment for this force and also beefed up the Assault Guards to 28,000 men. The *carabineros*, or customs guards, were increased to 40,000, many times their pre-war strength. The government hoped to use these forces in place of the army it still did not have, and also as a force that could counter the potentially revolutionary militias. The informal police squads formed by the various parties and unions were ordered into a new government-controlled "Vigilance Militia," a step designed to bring the terror under control.

By the beginning of October 1936 Largo Caballero became convinced of the ineffectiveness of the militias and moved to create a new Republican army. He decreed that the militias were to be under the orders of the central general staff and initiated a system of political commissars throughout the army, modeled after the successful system used by the communist Fifth Regiment. He formed—on paper, at least—"mixed brigades," or self-sufficient military units that were composed of militiamen, regular army soldiers, and new recruits and were commanded by army officers who would train them and maintain discipline.

But these steps were strongly resisted and Largo Caballero showed little inclination to exercise firm leadership. By the end of October the Republic had a more representative government, had taken some small steps that would eventually lead to a more capable army, had more or less ended the terror—and faced a powerful enemy now at the gates of Madrid.

# 5

# *Franco's Long March*

At first, they came across the Strait in a trickle, but then the big German transport planes flew more of Franco's soldiers to Spain, and by the beginning of August nearly 4,000 Moroccan and Foreign Legion troops were camping in Seville's parks and promenades.

Despite its name, the bulk of the Foreign Legion's forces were Spaniards, attracted by the spirit of comradeship and adventure in a self-contained world of lost, hardened men. The Legion was the most feared unit in the army, known for its readiness to kill in cold blood and for its habit of mutilating the corpses of its fallen enemies. These practices were encouraged by Franco when, in the 1920's, he led it in the Moroccan campaigns. In a memoir of those years, Franco described a typical action: "The job is difficult but pretty. . . . While one section opens fire on the houses . . . another slips down by a small cutting, surrounds the villages, and puts the inhabitants to the sword; the flames rise from the roofs of the houses and the legionnaires pursue their residents." Looting, rape, and murder followed.

The Moors, as the Moroccan troops were known, were mercenaries, natives hired to fight their countrymen for the greater glory of Spain's empire. They, too, enjoyed a reputa-

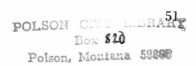
POLSON CITY LIBRARY
Box 820
Polson, Montana 59860

tion for brutality. It was common after a battle to find the turbaned Moors, their chests crisscrossed with cartridge belts, walking among the dead and wounded chipping out gold teeth with rocks and cutting fingers off to get rings. Many Spaniards, including some on the Nationalist side, were deeply disturbed by the use of Moorish troops, for modern Spain came into being only after the Catholic Reconquest of the fifteenth century had driven the Moors out of Spain. Now these Moslem warriors were called back to fight Spaniards again, this time as part of a self-styled "Christian Crusade."

Two main roads branched out of Seville toward Madrid. One, through Córdoba, was the shortest route to the capital, the one the Republic would expect the rebels to take. The other and longer route, through the city of Mérida, was the one Franco chose for his advance, partly because it was the quickest way to get the desperately needed small arms and ammunition to Mola's Army of the North, which held the territory to the north and west of Madrid. On August 3 1,500 Moors and legionnaires set out from Seville. After a lightning advance of eighty miles in two days, they ran into stiff resistance. Reinforced by another 1,500 men, the travel-weary fighters beat off a weak Republican army of militiamen and captured Mérida. It had taken only a week to reach a point halfway to Madrid.

The Army of Africa, commanded by Colonel Yagüe, now veered off to the west to attack the heavily fortified city of Badajoz, defended by more than 4,000 militiamen who had just put down an attempted rising by the Guardias. The old walled city near the Portuguese border stood astride a main north-south road, making it an important military objective, for its capture would mean direct contact with Mola's army without the international complications that might arise from using the territory of the friendly Portuguese.

The attack began on August 14, with artillery barrages on the thick impenetrable medieval walls of the city. One small band of attackers managed to fight their way into town from the rear, but the main force still faced sandbagged machine-gun nests at the parapets of the walls. Yagüe then ordered a direct assault on the city gates. After a small opening was made with dynamite, legionnaires sped toward the crackling machine guns in a suicidal rush. Over half of the first wave was cut down, but the survivors bayoneted their way past the gun emplacements and into the city, which they took after hours of hand-to-hand combat on the blood-spashed alleys and streets.

The horrors that followed shocked a world not yet hardened to the ferocity of total war. The bullring became the scene of nightly massacres. "They were young, mostly peasants in blue blouses, mechanics in jumpers," reported the American correspondent Jay Allen. "They are still being rounded up. At four o'clock in the morning they are turned out into the ring through the gate by which the initial parade of the bull-fight enters. There, machine guns await them. After the first night the blood was supposed to be palm deep at the far side of the lane." Up to 2,000 were killed in this way at the hot, dusty, tragic town of Badajoz.

At first, rebel officers were proud of the work their legion-naires did at Badajoz. But the wave of indignation that swept the civilized world in the wake of news reports from Ameri-can, French, and Portuguese journalists at the scene led to official denials that it had ever happened. Today, National-ist histories published in Spain claim that only a few hun-dred were killed at Badajoz, all in the battle for the city. But Yagüe defended the slaughter. "Of course we shot them," he told an American war correspondent. "What do you ex-pect? Was I supposed to take 4,000 Reds with me as my column advanced, racing against time? Was I supposed to turn them loose in my rear and let them make Badajoz Red again?"

But military necessity was not the only reason for the brutality. The Nationalists used terror as a means of intimidating their enemies; they believed they were fighting against an absolute evil that could only be eliminated by killing every single leftist they could get their hands on. For the Moors and the legionnaires, orders were orders. They, too, had demons of their own to conquer: fallen comrades had to be avenged, and the traditions of the savagely fought Moroccan wars were their inheritance. The end of the slaughter of battle was but a signal for a new slaughter to begin.

The advance north to Mérida and Badajoz, and then on to Talavera de la Reina farther up the Madrid road, left a bloody trail of bitter combat and vicious reprisals on both sides. The Legion's advance followed a regular pattern. Transported in trucks looted from conquered villages, with stolen articles tied securely to the roof and religious medallions hanging from the radiators, "flying squads" of 150 or so soldiers would drive up the Madrid road. Spying a village ahead, they would jump from the trucks, set up machine guns, and riddle the makeshift defenses of the militia. Sometimes they would radio for air support, and a slow, heavy plane would appear overhead, lob a few bombs over its side, and fly off. Ineffective as such bombing raids were, they panicked even militiamen who would brave bayonet charges and fight with knives at close quarters. The untrained amateur soldiers bunched up in their trenches at the sight of an airplane, and the first bomb that plopped harmlessly into the nearby fields would send them scurrying out of their shelters and into the open road. There, they were shot down like rabbits. The victorious legionnaires would then enter the village and plunder it. Loading their trucks with more booty, the deathly caravan would proceed on to the next village, leaving behind a small detachment of volunteers, usually local Falangists and soldiers, to keep the village under rebel control and to finish off the deadly business of killing their enemies.

Anyone who carried a union card, was known to be a member of a left-wing party, or had been heard to make disrespectful remarks against the Church or the army was fair game for the firing squads. In the days following the fall of a village, men and women would be stopped on the streets and ordered to bare their shoulders. If they had the telltale blue bruises that indicated they had fired a rifle recently, they were shot. "There seemed no end to the killing," reported newsman John T. Whitaker. "They were shooting as many at the end of the second month as in my first days in Talavera. They averaged perhaps thirty a day. . . . And there were mopping-up operations along the roads. You would find three or four old peasant women heaped in a ditch; thirty and forty militiamen at a time, their hands roped behind them, shot down at the crossroads." In Santa Olalla, Whitaker observed a mass execution—some six hundred Republican militiamen herded into the town square and mowed down by machine guns.

In this way, by early September Franco's armies had cut a wide swath through the Republic's territory. They conquered the radical region of Estremadura, were masters of a good part of Andalusia, had swept away the Republic's counterattacks, and were now speeding up the Madrid road toward an apparently defenseless capital.

While attention was riveted on the speedy advances of the Franco armies, the rebels were making gains in the north, too. Accepting a stalemate in the mountain passes above Madrid, where thinly manned militia units of both sides skirmished to no clear result, Mola decided to attack the Basque province of Guipúzcoa. Shortly after the July revolt Carlist militia from Navarre threw themselves upon their fellow Catholic Basque neighbors. Early in August, Mola began an offensive to cut the Basque border with France. His main targets were the border town of Irún and the summer capital of Spain, the fashionable resort city of San Sebastián, on the Bay of Biscay.

From August 17 on, the few ships under rebel command bombarded San Sebastián from the sea, while Italian planes ran daily bombing missions. On the 26th Mola launched the attack on Irún with 2,000 troops and every heavy gun his army had. Rebel artillery mercilessly shelled Basque positions, then infantry swept in to take them. After regrouping, the Basque defenders would rush back to recapture. The seesaw struggle continued, but the rebels slowly crawled forward, tightening the noose around Irún. By the beginning of September they were on the heights overlooking the city, and the people of Irún fled across the frontier, taking with them everything they could carry on their backs or in carts, for they knew that even if they would be able to return to their homes, the battle would wreck the town. From the heights on the French side of the border they watched their city die. After beating off a rebel attack, most of the outgunned defenders retreated to San Sebastián or fled across the border, leaving the town in the hands of a rearguard Anarchist militia which set it on fire. When the rebel victors entered Irún on September 4, they occupied a charred ruin.

On that same day Franco's troops entered Talavera de la Reina, a key city on the route to Madrid. On the previous day, September 3, a small Catalan invading force in Majorca was forced to flee the island before a ferocious counter-attack supported by Italian bombers that left many of their men dead on the sand-swept beaches. On September 8 units of the Armies of the North and the South met in the mountains southwest of Madrid, unifying the rebel forces. In Andalusia they extended their thrust into Republican territory and now held the hills behind Málaga. On the 13th the Basque defenders of San Sebastián, refusing to allow the city to be destroyed like Irún, surrendered.

In the first two months of the war, then, the unbroken string of rebel victories brought almost half of Spain under their control and, now, Franco's armies rapidly neared the capital, Madrid, for what they thought would be the final thrust of the war. Following a rest period in which they were heavily reinforced by fresh legionnaires brought from Morocco, Franco's army resumed its triumphant march north. Then, on September 23, it was ordered to halt the drive on Madrid and detour to Toledo, where one of the most dramatic incidents of the entire war was being played out—the siege of the Alcázar.

Toledo, only about thirty miles south of Madrid, had been in Republican hands since the failure of the July rebellion there. In the heart of this ancient city, on a high bluff overlooking the Tagus River, squatted a huge, turreted, thick-walled fortress, the Alcázar. Inside the building, which had been Spain's military academy, were 2,000 Guardias, soldiers, cadets, and Falangists, their families, and some 250 left-wing hostages, all under the command of Colonel José Moscardó. When his rebellion failed, Colonel Moscardó retreated behind the thick walls of the Alcázar, and for the next ten weeks his band of rebels withstood bombs, dynamite attacks, and constant artillery shelling to capture the imagination of Nationalist Spain and the grudging admiration of many Republicans as well.

At first, the Republicans decided to wait things out, expecting Moscardó to realize he was trapped and surrender. On July 23 the head of the Toledo militia telephoned him to say that his son, Luis, was a captive and would be shot if the

Alcázar did not surrender in ten minutes. Refusing to believe him, Moscardó then heard the voice of his son on the phone. "They say if you don't surrender, they will shoot me," the young man told his father. "Well then," the colonel answered, "commend your soul to God and die like a true patriot crying 'Long live Christ, the King' and 'Long live Spain.' "

Moscardó's sacrifice electrified the defenders and helped imbue the spirit of resistance that enabled them to withstand the difficult days that followed. Their dwindling food supply was rationed, then all but vanished. Sanitary conditions deteriorated, worsened by the need to huddle in the dank cellars to avoid the constant shellings. The Republic's planes regularly circled overhead, their bombs doing only minimal damage to the sturdy building. Militiamen filled nearby windows and rooftops, pumping round after round into its walls. From a hill across the river, artillery units pummeled it. At night, bright floodlights played on the ghostly hulk as the shelling continued. Madrileños journeyed down from the capital on Sundays to join in the firing or to picnic on the grass alongside the heavy guns, cheering each salvo. Still, the massive fortress held out.

Then, miners were brought from Asturias. They burrowed underneath the fortress and set off powerful charges that blanketed Toledo in massive clouds of black smoke. The explosion was heard as far away as Madrid's suburbs. Miraculously, the defenders were still able to beat off militiamen scrambling through the ruins with flame throwers and rifles. Only one of the Alcázar's four towers still stood, huge holes were blown in its thick walls, and its defenders were half-starved ghosts; but still the militia could not capture it.

Franco had to decide whether to relieve the defenders or push on to the capital. It seemed likely that Moscardó's be-

leaguered garrison would fall before help arrived, and purely
military considerations argued for continuing the drive on
Madrid. But Franco had given his word to the defenders, and
the decision was made to relieve the Alcázar. "In all wars,
and above all in civil wars," Franco said, "morale factors
count to an extraordinary degree. We have to impress the
enemy by convincing him that whatever we propose to do we
achieve and they can't do anything to stop it."

On September 23 a relief force under the command of
General José Enrique Varela set out for Toledo. And two
days later, Nationalist planes and heavy guns were shelling the Republican artillery positions. On the 26th a rebel
detachment circled around the city and cut off the road
to Madrid, trapping the militia within the city. On the morning of the 27th, with Varela only four miles outside the city,
an explosion ripped the air and a plume of black smoke
rose above the fortress. It was another mine—the last, vain
attempt to destroy the Alcázar. By midday the first Moorish
troops were entering the city and rebel planes were firing on
the militiamen running from Toledo on the open roads. Before nightfall the survivors of the siege ordeal staggered
out into the twilight, tears of relief running down their faces.
On the 28th Varela climbed over the rubble of what was left
of the Alcázar and was met by Moscardó, whose first words
were *"sin novedad en el Alcázar,"* "nothing new in the Alcázar."

Nationalist vengeance was swift and horrible. Varela ordered no prisoners taken, and his forces enthusiastically went
on a rampage. Moscardó's hostages were shot. Moors invaded
the hospital and bayoneted wounded militiamen in their
beds. The stones of the Zocodover, one of Spain's most beauti-
ful squares, just down the hill from the Alcázar, ran red with
blood.

On September 29 Franco arrived to pin a medal on Moscardó and to honor the brave defenders of the Alcazar, who stood with eyes blinking against the unfamiliar sun, their gaunt looks and weakened bodies testifying to the terrible ordeal they had survived.

"Now," a beaming Franco told reporters, "the war is won."

# 6

# *The World and the War*

Like a stone thrown into a stagnant pool, the ripples of Spain's civil war spread outward beyond its border. Europe was tense with war scares at the time. Nazi Germany, fresh from occupying the Rhineland in violation of its treaties, was re-arming feverishly. Italy's conquest of Ethiopia whetted Mussolini's appetite for more. Dictatorships, fascism, and aggressive wars and threats of wars were sprouting throughout the world. It was into this troubled global scene that the Spanish Civil War burst in 1936. Some European statesmen feared it might become the spark that would set off World War II, but others looked on it as a stroke of luck, for it fit their plans perfectly.

Nazi Germany, preparing for a war of domination, was one of these. Field Marshall Goering told the Nuremberg war crimes trial in 1946 that when Franco's first request for aid came, he urged Hitler to comply, for he eagerly sought "this opportunity to test my young Luftwaffe in this or that technical respect." The German tank commander, General von Thoma, saw that "Spain would serve as the European Aldershot," or training grounds, and rushed to Spain with specialists who "were used to train Franco's tank forces—and to get battle experience themselves."

While German transport planes were airlifting rebel troops

to mainland Spain and a shipload of fighter planes and technicians neared Cádiz, the German foreign minister was telling the French ambassador that his country "naturally did not intervene in Spanish internal political affairs and disputes." In early November German aid was stepped up to include the Condor Legion of about a hundred bombers and fighter planes, anti-aircraft and anti-tank units, tanks, and military specialists. German warships operated in Spanish waters. Modern planes and tanks were shipped to Spain as fast as new models rolled off the assembly lines. Almost as important as this military muscle was the officer-training program the Germans set up to help supply the rebel armies with new stocks of well-trained leaders in the field. German aid eventually amounted to a quarter of a billion dollars' worth of weapons, and at any given moment during the war there were 6,500 German fliers, tank crews, and military advisers in Spain.

Despite this, German aid was still not large enough to ensure a swift Nationalist victory. This was by design, for Hitler preferred a drawn-out war. "A one hundred percent Franco victory is not desirable," he told his aides. "We are more interested in a continuation of the war and preservation of tensions in the Mediterranean." Civil war in Spain was useful as a diversion that concentrated the attention of the democracies on the boiling Spanish pot, freeing Hitler's hand for activities elsewhere. At the same time, Hitler wanted Franco to win eventually, for he needed Spain in friendly hands when the war Germany was preparing for finally came. With a Spanish ally, Hitler could control the western Mediterranean and endanger Britain's sea routes. Germany also wanted the rich lodes of iron ore and other minerals in Spain and in her Moroccan colony, which helped pay for the German aid.

Strict limits were placed on this aid. Hitler did not want to get bogged down in an endless war in Spain; he had bigger fish to fry. Above all, he wanted Spain to generate tensions, not a premature war with France and England. So he never publicly admitted his aid to Franco until after the end of the civil war, and German "volunteers" traveled to Spain disguised as tourists. Some just disappeared from their military units, to return, with a Spanish sun tan, six months later.

The fledgling alliance between Hitler and Mussolini was cemented by their cooperation in helping Franco, and the Germans actively encouraged Italy to take the major role in Spain. Mussolini wanted to make Italy the dominant power in the Mediterranean and a friendly Spain was essential for this. His feuds with France and England threatened to erupt into a war in which a Spanish ally would be invaluable. Above all, Spain offered another opportunity to demonstrate Italy's new military power. "When the war in Spain is over, I shall have to find something else," he said. "The Italian character has to be formed through fighting."

Spain became Italy's Vietnam, a never-ending cesspool that drained its strength, chewed up its shallow reserves of war materials, and offered nothing tangible in return. Franco merely exchanged promises of future support for Rome's ambitions in the Mediterranean in return for immediate deliveries of arms and front-line soldiers. By the beginning of 1937 14,000 Italians were fighting in Franco's army, with many thousands more to follow. The dozen planes Mussolini sent Franco in July 1936 to help transport the army from Morocco grew to become an investment of almost 800 airplanes, vehicles, guns, and ammunition worth some $400 million, and the lives of 6,000 Italians who fell in battle.

Neighboring Portugal also leaped to Franco's aid. Republicans who managed to escape across the border were returned to face certain death at the hands of the rebels. Several thousand Portuguese fought in Franco's army. German arms were often unloaded in Lisbon, then shipped across the border to the Nationalists.

The dictators rushed to help the rebels, but the democracies, imprisoned by their fear of a general war, refused to aid the Republic, thus condemning it to defeat. As the Chilean poet Pablo Neruda wrote:

> . . . Spain tore the earth with her nails
> When Paris was prettier than ever.
> Spain drained her immense tree of blood
> When London was grooming . . . her lawn and
> her swan lakes . . .

The Republic turned first to France, a friendly country whose Popular Front government understood the danger to France's rear of a Spain beholden to the Germans and Italians. But France was weak and her foreign policy was based on alliance with Britain. When Prime Minister Léon Blum received the Republic's call for help on July 20, while the outcome of the rebellion was still in doubt and fighting was still going on in Madrid and Barcelona, he immediately agreed to send arms. But his British allies intervened. Summoned to London, Blum was warned that France would have to stand alone if her intervention in Spain led to war. This threat, along with shrill opposition from the French Right, chilled the Cabinet. "My soul is torn," Blum told the Spanish ambassador in a tearful interview. On July 25 the French rejected plans to aid Spain, but arranged for covert help for private sales of arms. Then the British, after slapping an embargo on all arms sales to either side, tightened the screws on the French. On August 8 Blum closed the border with Spain and, except for sporadic occasions when it temporarily suited French policy to let aid through, the border stayed sealed, and with it, the fate of the Republic.

England's Conservative government was more comfortable with the rebels than with a leftist regime that might threaten British control over some sectors of Spain's economy. But her overriding interest lay in confining the war to Spain and to keep it from flaring into a general war. Britain's policy of appeasement, a process of compromise to lessen tensions and avoid war, was designed to keep Europe from splitting into two hostile blocs. Hitler was viewed as a rather nasty individual who might yet be brought around to act like a gentleman. Hovering above the diplomats of the democracies was the ghost of World War I and the terrible memories of the millions dead in its four years of trench warfare. They were prepared to do anything to avoid another such catastrophe.

Pressured by the British, Blum proposed that all of Europe's powers sign a Non-Intervention Agreement pledging to stay out of the conflict and not to help either side. August 1936 was a month of frantic diplomacy to reach an international agreement on non-intervention. By the end of the month, while shipping aid to Franco and sending him pilots and technicians, Germany and Italy signed the agreement, considering it no more than a worthless piece of paper. On September 9 a Non-Intervention Committee made up of ambassadors of the signatories began regular meetings in London to supervise the agreement.

The United States did not sign the agreement, for it already had a strict policy of isolationism aimed at keeping the country out of any future wars. Congress rushed through a special law in January 1937 barring arms sales to either side in the Spanish conflict. The embargo had loopholes in it, for it allowed certain kinds of war materials to be sold, and Franco bought more than 12,000 trucks from Ford and General Motors at inflated prices. Texaco shipped oil to the rebels, much of it on credit, which was illegal, for the law said that all sales to war areas had to be on a cash basis.

Most Americans approved the embargo. Although the Republic's supporters outnumbered those of the rebels, the average citizen favored neutrality. Some Catholics agreed with the young John F. Kennedy, who wrote after a visit to Spain, "the government was in the right morally speaking," and praised its religious policies. Catholic opinion was divided, with only a large minority supporting Franco, but this included the politically powerful lay organizations and Church hierarchy, which influenced national policy. The Hearst newspaper chain helped foster pro-Franco opinion by labeling government forces "reds" and rebels "Nationalists" in their news columns. And when a *New York Times* reporter sent word of Italian troops in the front lines, editors back home changed his reference to read "rebel troops," thus helping to hide the facts about Italy's intervention.

Except for Mexico, which sent what little arms and ammunition it could afford, which wasn't much, the only country to help the Republic was Russia. Even this aid was not forthcoming immediately, for Stalin was very cautious. Russian policy was tied to hopes of a military alliance with France and England to contain Nazi Germany. By 1936 Communist propaganda for world revolution had given way to calls for a united front of all people against fascism. Russia did not want to antagonize France and England, so it limited itself to sending food and medical supplies to the Republic. On August 23 Russia signed the Non-Intervention Agreement and reluctantly prepared to follow a hands-off policy in Spain.

But continued German and Italian aid to the rebels led Stalin to change his position. By the beginning of September the network of undercover Communist agents throughout Europe was ordered to buy arms for shipment to Spain. In October, with the Non-Intervention Committee refusing to stop German, Italian, and Portuguese aid to the rebels, Russia announced it would not be bound by the agreement "in any greater measure than any of the other participants." Stalin now started direct military aid to the Republic.

By mid-October the first Russian tanks and planes arrived and were immediately pressed into service on the Madrid front. With them came army advisers, tank specialists, and fliers. These Russians, who never numbered more than five hundred at any one time, were under Stalin's orders to "stay out of range of artillery fire." The Russian dictator did not want to lose his badly needed military experts on Spanish battlefields, nor did he want to worsen relations with the French and British by advertising Russia's direct involvement in the fighting.

The Russians in Spain were a mysterious lot; they used false names and, as one observer reported, kept "in monastic seclusion and absolute separation from the rest of the government troops." Except for tank crews and fliers, they stayed well behind the front lines, dealing directly with high Spanish officers. As the Republic's dependence on their aid increased, the Russians' power grew and few major military decisions were made without their approval, Stalin's aid had a high price tag: about $600 million in gold was shipped to Russia for safekeeping, and it eventually paid the bills for military hardware and other aid.

Like Hitler, Stalin did not want a quick, clear-cut victory for his side. Russian policy was aimed at reaching a collective-security alliance with the democracies to contain Hitler, and he wanted to keep the Republic alive at least long enough for the French and British to come to their senses and understand the threat to their own security if Spain fell because of the Axis intervention.

But it wasn't until 1939 that the democracies finally understood that they could not do business with Hitler. In the meantime they clung to the policy of appeasement, and the only diplomatic result of Russia's intervention was to bring upon itself the wrath of the Non-Intervention Committee. While the committee carefully looked the other way when complaints of German and Italian intervention were made, it swiftly condemned Russia's help to the Republic.

Since the committee had no powers, it could only expose violations of the agreement, something that would hardly deter Hitler or Mussolini. As a result, it functioned as a screen behind which nations intervened at will. The Nazi representative, von Ribbentrop, joked that its name ought to have been changed to "the intervention committee." The League of Nations also proved powerless, and its inability to deal with the Spanish conflict helped discredit it. The universal hands-off policy regarding Spain was a gross breach of established international practice. As the Russian newspaper *Izvestia* editorialized: "Up to the present time there has been no precedent whereby the government of any country elected in accordance with its laws and recognized by all powers is put on a level both judicially and in practice with rebels fighting it."

The committee went through the motions of pretending to stop intervention. It occasionally cited violators, and it held regular, lengthy meetings that solved nothing. Franco's backers on the committee worked together to delay proceedings and to cover each other's tracks. In March 1937 the committee agreed on a "control plan" that extended the farce of non-intervention. By placing land observers on Spain's borders and instituting sea patrols of the great powers, it would detect violations of the agreement. If observers discovered arms shipments, they would report to London and the committee would inform the offending government. Not only were no sanctions provided for, but Germany and Italy were assigned to be part of the sea patrol, so the violators were also the policemen. The only result of the control plan was to ensure that no aid to the Republic leaked through the French border, while Franco continued to get help from Germany and Italy. The committee limped through the rest of the war in this farcical manner.

If the nations of the world were ready to abandon the Republic, many of their citizens were not. All over the world feelings of idealism and hunger for adventure were unleashed by the plight of the liberal Republic fighting for its life against army rebels supported by Hitler and Mussolini. Spain became "the last great cause," the last worldwide event that spurred people to believe they must fight and die, if necessary, for ideals of liberty. "If you had asked me why I had joined the militia," wrote George Orwell, "I should have answered: 'To fight against Fascism,' and if you had asked me what I was fighting *for*, I should have answered: 'Common decency.'"

No sooner did the fighting start than volunteers began to arrive in Spain. The French writer André Malraux organized an air squadron, and German and Italian political exiles enlisted in the militias or formed units of their own. These volunteers fought at Irún, joined the Catalan Anarchist's march to the Aragon front, and dug trenches in Madrid. W. H. Auden captured the spirit with which foreigners rushed to Spain when he wrote:

> They clung like burrs to the long expresses that lurch
> Through the unjust lands, through the night,
> > through the alpine tunnel;
> They floated over the oceans;
> They walked the passes; they came to present their lives.

By mid-October the government decided to organize the foreign volunteers into an International Brigade. The Communists helped recruit volunteers in several countries, and Josip Broz, later to become famous as Yugoslavia's Marshal Tito, ran an underground railroad operation from Paris that smuggled volunteers into Spain. A training base was established at a dusty provincial town, Albacete, halfway between Madrid and Valencia. André Marty, a French Communist, was placed in charge of the camp, and his violent behavior and paranoid fear of spies earned him the title of "The Butcher of Albacete." The Russians provided the military heads of the new unit, and these included more mystery men: soldiers like its commander, General Emil Kleber, whose real name is thought to have been Gregory Stern, a veteran of fighting with Mao in China. There were others with assumed names who later surfaced as important leaders of Communist parties in France, Italy, Trieste, and elsewhere. The majority of the volunteers were not Communists; rather, they were idealists who believed they were fighting for democracy and against the Fascist menace to the freedom of their home countries.

Some 35,000 people from fifty-three countries served in the International Brigades during the course of the war, but there were never more than 6,000 at the front at any one time. These foreign troops fighting for the Republic were outnumbered by the 130,000 Moroccans, Italians, Germans, and Portuguese who fought for the rebels. Used as shock troops in the Republic's most hard-fought campaigns, the Internationals took terrible casualties. About a third of the 10,000 French volunteers, two out of five of the 5,000 German and Austrian exiles, and almost a third of the roughly 3,000 Americans were killed.

The first Americans arrived in January 1937. The government outlawed recruiting for volunteers and stamped all passports "Not valid for Spain." But still they came, secretly recruited by Communist organizations, supplied with goods bought at army surplus stores, and shipped to France as "tourists." The lucky ones took the train across the border, but since the French border was sealed for most of the war, they were more often smuggled across the Pyrenees, struggling to keep up with their guides along the treacherous mountain paths. They came from all walks of life: the largest single group were seamen; most of the rest were students, laborers, and unionists. The rain, wind, and bitter cold that hampered their journey did not stop them, for they came to "present their lives" in a cause that gripped their souls.

# 7

# *The Battle for Madrid*

By late October 1936 the Army of Africa had advanced to the outskirts of Madrid. They swept through villages on the roads to the capital, beating off determined but ineffective militia resistance. About 25,000 men, the cream of the rebel forces, spearheaded the attack on Madrid, commanded by General Varela and under the overall direction of General Mola. Mola pinned his hopes of victory on the fighting power of his small army, on a campaign of terror that would paralyze popular resistance, and on the support of rebel sympathizers within the city who would support the troops once they pierced its weak defenses. It was this large corps of secret pro-Nationalists to which Mola referred when he said that the city would be taken not by the four army columns marching on it but by the "fifth column" within it, a phrase that has meant treachery and espionage ever since.

The rebel attack was slowed by the timely arrival of the first Russian tanks, which were immediately rushed into action. On the 29th they plowed through Moroccan cavalry but had to retreat with heavy losses when the foot soldiers of the Loyalist's Fifth Regiment could not keep pace with them. They did convince the rebel command, however, that Madrid was too heavily defended on its southern approaches, and

Mola shifted his forces for an attack from the southwest.

First, the rebels launched a campaign of airborne terror, designed to frighten Madrid into submission. On October 23 the first German Junker bombers raided the city, and by October 30 Madrid suffered daily air attacks. That day six heavy bombers attacked the suburb of Getafe, killing sixty children. The next day the bombers claimed higher casualties. Mola broadcast that 150,000 rebel troops were attacking Madrid; Italian planes dropped leaflets warning that if the city did not surrender "Nationalist aviation will wipe it from the earth"; and messages from Franco were dropped calling the militia to "Throw down your arms and free yourselves from the lying leaders who deceive you." Still, the bombs fell on Madrid's civilian population and on the thousands of refugees who had crowded into the capital to escape the advancing rebels.

On November 4 the rebels took the virtually undefended airport at Getafe and occupied other nearby suburbs. That same day, the Republican Cabinet was reorganized to include four anarchists, thus completing the show of unity. But the rebel advance continued. British and French diplomats wired their governments that Madrid might fall momentarily. The rebels appointed civil officials for the city, stored food and supplies to be distributed, and announced the official marching order of the victory parade. More ominously, they assigned boundaries of operation to the squads of Falangists who would round up political enemies.

On November 6 the government decided to abandon Madrid. The official explanation was that the government could not function in a war zone, but actually, Largo Caballero was convinced that Madrid was about to fall. Valencia was chosen as the new capital, and after turning over command of Madrid's defenses to the elderly General José Miaja,

Largo and the other high officials piled into waiting auto-mobiles with their files and hurried away along the Valencia road before it could be cut by the rebels. On the way, the ministers were stopped by the "Iron Column," a band of Anarchist militia, who ordered them at gunpoint to return to Madrid. They faked their way past the partisan guards and rushed off into the night to the safety of Valencia.

In Madrid the hapless General Miaja realized he had been selected to surrender the capital, not to save it. On the evening of the 6th, while the Cabinet sped away from the dying city, Miaja and General Sebastián Pozas were handed their orders. Fortunately, the generals opened their sealed envelopes at once, instead of waiting until the morning as instructed. Each set of instructions had been placed in the wrong envelope: in Miaja's were the orders commanding Pozas to organize a new headquarters for the central army outside Madrid; in Pozas' were instructions for Miaja to organize a defense junta to coordinate Madrid's last stand. Had they separated and waited until morning, Madrid would have been in total chaos.

The situation was grim enough. Miaja was left on his own with no government to help him. Military files were on the road to Valencia, and he discovered the retreat orders to the militia guarding the passes above Madrid just in time to cancel them, saving a vital defense point that could have caused the city to fall. As word of the government's flight spread to the frightened city, other officials joined the caravan to safety. Maddened by the imminent arrival of the rebels, prison guards took vengeance on right-wing political prisoners and slaughtered them. The smell of fear was in the air, and across the river General Varela, informed that Miaja was now in charge of Madrid, laughed, "He is a poor old grandpa, we will beat him easily."

But the old general was determined to go down fighting. He quickly assembled a staff of officers headed by Lieutenant Colonel Vicente Rojo, one of the most respected younger officers in the pre-war army. Their first task was to re-establish contact with the scattered militia units at the front and to hunt up ammunition. Miaja summoned officers, union leaders, and political party activists in the War Ministry, where he told them, "I want men with me who know how to die." Then they went into the tense night streets of Madrid to organize the defense of the city. Military lines of communication were established and the people were organized on a block-by-block basis to resist.

La Pasionaria's voice was heard on the government radio imploring Madrileños to fight to their last ounce of strength. Her slogans were picked up and chanted by groups all over the city: "It is better to die on your feet than live on your knees"; "It is better to be the widow of a hero than the wife of a coward"; and the inevitable "No paseran!" Huge posters proclaimed that "Madrid shall be the tomb of fascism," and the city was flooded with leaflets demanding, "Let every house be a fortress," with instructions on how to make homemade gasoline bombs to throw at tanks. With their backs to the wall, the people of Madrid now prepared to make the rebels pay in blood for every street, every stone of their beloved city.

The long-awaited attack broke at dawn on the morning of November 7. As the shells of Varela's heavy artillery pummeled the southwestern stretches of the city, unarmed workers rushed to the front, and women and children piled stone upon stone to barricade the streets. The rebels' plan of attack was to cross the Manzanares River running between the Casa de Campo and the streets of the city, climb uphill to capture the prison, the barracks, and the buildings of University City, and from these vantage points within Madrid pour fire into the Plaza de España and Madrid's Broadway, the Gran Vía.

Against the powerful guns and the tough soldiers of the Army of Africa, Madrid had only her people, civilians whose few guns had barely enough ammunition, civilians who were willing to die now at their posts rather than fall victims to the extermination squads of the victorious rebels. The fighting was ferocious. In the battle for Toledo Bridge, south of the Casa de Campo, an entire company of militia was wiped out, and the Legion found itself in hand-to-hand combat with a unit of militiawomen. "Going up to the line were long files of civilians," reported an English observer. "They had no uniforms. Just ordinary suits and a rifle slung anyhow over the shoulder. Most of the rifles were aged and I should say were nearly as unsafe for the man who fired as for the enemy." Some civilians rushed to the front without any weapons at all, hoping to pick up the guns of fallen defenders, while others went to the front without ammunition for their guns.

Through the chaos of battle, Miaja sat among the jangling phones in his War Ministry office, giving orders and calming frantic front-line officers pleading for reinforcements and ammunition. He had neither, but the elderly general calmly promised everyone that reinforcements were on the way or that trucks of ammunition would arrive momentarily. Hold on, he told them, just another forty-eight hours and we will have won. Varela urged his men on with increasing frenzy. By nightfall few of the first day's objectives had been won; losses were heavy and the apparently undefended city was proving a formidable target.

At nine that night, militiamen blew up a rebel tank on one of the roads on the outskirts of Madrid. When they inspected the inside of the charred hulk, they found the body of the commander of the armored forces of the rebel army, and the official-looking documents they tore from his jacket pocket were sent to Miaja. They were Varela's battle orders for the day. The defenders now knew exactly what paths the rebel columns planned to take. When Varela's troops tried to attack the next morning, they found the Republic's few guns concentrated on their line of advance.

Varela now changed his plans. He ordered his Moroccan troops to take the Model Prison at all costs. Backed by withering artillery support, they charged across the river and, despite heavy losses, broke through the militia lines. Miaja rushed to the front, saw his troops retreating and whipped out his pistol, climbed over the debris left by the heavy shelling, and screamed at his men: "Cowards! Cowards! Die in your trenches! Die with your General Miaja!" As his staff dragged Miaja away, the chastened troops turned back to face the drawn bayonets of the invaders. Their lines held this time, and the attack was beaten off. But Miaja knew he could not ask the impossible forever; sooner or later the superior firepower of the rebels would shatter the thin lines of defenders. Already, congratulatory telegrams addressed to General Franco were arriving at the War Ministry. The rebels fought their way up the Garabitas Heights in the Casa de Campo and their heavy guns now brought the whole city under fire.

Around noon on November 8 the crowds along the Gran Vía could hear the bursting shells and constant gunfire at the front, only a short walk away. Then these sounds of war were mixed with other sounds—the sounds of boots slapping against the pavement and clipped orders shouted in a strange tongue. Marching down the Gran Vía were the first of 3,000 soldiers of the International Brigade, rushed from their training camp at Albacete to help the defenders of Madrid. By evening French, German, and Polish volunteers were setting up their machine guns in University City and were spread out among the weary militiamen in the Casa de Campo. There, the Internationals, many of them veterans of the First World War, inspired the militiamen and showed them how to find the best gun positions and the importance of digging foxholes.

When Varela's troops resumed the attack on the 9th, they were met with more accurate fire than they had ever experienced, as the guns of the International Brigade cut down the rebel fighters. Still, the attack pressed on. Key positions were won, lost, won again, and then recaptured by the militia. Neither side let heavy losses slow the blistering pace of the fighting. The rebels completed their occupation of the Garabitas Heights and now began a breakthrough that might carry them into the city. General Kleber, the commander of the Internationals, pulled his forces together to meet the threat. As night fell, the volunteers counter-attacked among the ilex and gum trees of the Casa de Campo. By morning the rebels had been cleared from the park and held only the Heights, but a third of the Internationals lay dead on the blood-soaked grassy slopes.

The back of the rebel attack was broken, and Varela shifted his main offensive to the south, where, in the slum district of Carabanchel Bajo, Moroccan soldiers fought among the shattered ruins of houses against the rifles and grenades of the forces led by "El Campesino," the Peasant. Savage fighting forced the defenders to retreat, but they had inflicted so much damage that the exhausted rebel troops had to stop. On the following days the opposing armies jockeyed for position and dug in for the next phase of the battle.

On November 14 the 3,000 Anarchist militiamen of the Catalonian hero Buenaventura Durruti marched down the Gran Vía to the cheers of crowds hailing this new, powerful addition to the city's defenses. Proud of his men, who had conquered much of Aragon, Durruti asked for an independent front. His troops were installed in a key sector of the Casa de Campo, just below the buildings of University City. Supported by the meager Republican artillery, Durruti launched an attack on the 15th, but the withering fire of the Moroccan machine guns pinned down his undisciplined troops. A counter-attack by the rebels reached the Manzanares River. Three times the rebels reached the river, three times they were beaten back. Then, with German bombers and heavy artillery supporting them, a shock force breached the river. The Anarchists fled in disorder, and the Army of Africa dashed up the hill to capture the buildings of the university. From the university buildings, the rebels looked down the broad avenues leading to the heart of Madrid. The Internationals were rushed to the scene and stopped the rebel advance, recapturing the Hall of Philosophy. More rebel troops poured through the breach in the defenses to join the struggle for the shattered buildings of University City.

While the opposing forces were locked in combat, rebel artillery systematically shelled the city, and German bombers dropped their death loads on civilian targets, including a hospital that had a huge red cross painted on its roof. In the next days the bombings continued at a heavier pace. The German pilots were guided by the fires along the Gran Vía caused by artillery shellings that blasted buildings and hit key plazas such as the Puerta del Sol and the Plaza de España. The barrages sometimes reached a peak of 2,000 shells per hour. The terrible raids brought heavy civilian casualties, and the sorely tested morale of the population was not improved by the leaflets showered on the stricken city on the morning of the 17th, leaflets that warned: "Unless the city surrenders by four o'clock this afternoon, bombardments will begin in earnest." That afternoon, the Puerta del Sol was fire-bombed again, and the flames danced their way across the historic old buildings of the section, leaving smoldering embers glowing in the ashes of Madrid's night. More than a thousand people died in the four days and nights of bombing from November 16 to 19.

Meanwhile, the battle for University City raged. Troops threw up barricades of philosophy books and poked rifles through windows, and grenades whistled across the spaces between buildings held by the opposing camps. Some buildings were shared by both rebels and defenders. Grenades were placed in service elevators and exploded when they reached the floor of the enemy. Moroccans in the Medical College's laboratories ate experimental animals and died. On the 17th the rebels broke through once more and the fleeing militia raced toward the Plaza de España. Once again, Miaja, gun in hand, challenged them back to battle and the crisis was met. That night five hundred more civilians were killed in bombing raids. For another week the buildings of University City were raked by sniper fire, shaken by grenades, and pounded by dynamite charges. By November 23 both sides, exhausted, broke off the fighting.

The rebels, expecting an easy conquest of a barely defended city, had been beaten off by the almost unbelievable will to resist of Madrid's common people, aided by the handful of international volunteers and inspired by the newly-found magnetism of an aging general. The rebels still held part of University City and had a bridgehead just below it. Their guns were perched on the Garabitas Heights. Their army blanketed the roads south and west of the city. But Madrid was still in Loyalist hands. Its people had survived the onslaughts of the Army of Africa. "This is Madrid," crackled the government radio station. "It is fighting for Spain, for

Humanity, for Justice. With the mantle of its blood, it shelters all human beings! Madrid! Madrid!"

Madrid was saved, but rebel armies still held fast to positions on three sides of the city, and the trenches and barbed wire crept along the border of the capital and, in some places, within the city itself. The fighting stopped, but the bombing didn't. The Germans were testing their policy of terror raids on civilian populations to break their will—a technique they later employed during World War II with raids that destroyed Coventry and Rotterdam. The Nationalists, cheated of the coveted capital, vented their fury with German bombs. The heroism of the November resistance gave way to the gray sullenness of siege.

Twenty thousand refugees camped in the streets and in the subways. A constant flow of people streamed toward the Chamartin quarter where foreign embassies were concentrated and the adjoining Salamanca district of upper-middle-class residences, because Franco announced he would not bomb those areas. With the rest of Madrid under constant air attack, people crowded the pavements and doorways of the favored areas, hoping to avoid the bombs. Louis Delaprée, a French journalist, reported that "these migrating tribes" made their way through the streets of Madrid "by whole families. The fathers walk ahead, carrying the mattresses on their heads. Behind them the children splashing in the muddy streets, without a laugh, without a smile, with somnambulists' eyes, with worn-out faces of little old men. Women constitute the rear guard, dragging handcarts full of old things, baskets, chairs and cages." They bless the rain, he reported, "for when the sun will reappear, the planes will also come back again. The most frightful, strange and sinister thing that I have seen in Madrid is this: thousands of men, women, and children who fear the return of the sun like the man condemned to death in his last night's cell."

The heavy bombs ripped ten-story buildings in half and sometimes even penetrated into the subway shelters. What the bombers did not destroy, the rebel artillery did. Every morning at seven their batteries opened up in what Madrileños came to call "the alarm clock." The Gran Vía, normally the city's most crowded street, with people thronging its shops and cafés, was blasted regularly.

The people of Madrid came to live with the bombs. Life went on. Foreign reporters accurately wired home that the terror had failed; instead of panic, a mood of resistance and courage took root. A kind of black humor thrived: refering to Mola's early October promise that in a week he would be drinking coffee on the Gran Vía, a café there placed a sign on its choice table, "Reserved for General Mola." The piercing chill howling down from the mountains was as much an enemy as the bombs. People risked their lives for wood to burn in the coal-less city. "It is a common sight," Herbert Matthews reported to *The New York Times*, "to see men, women and children foraging among the ruins of houses for parts of beams, pieces of flooring, broken furniture—anything so long as it is wood and will burn."

Madrid was a hungry city, too. Long lines formed outside shops, people clutching their ration books in the hopes of finding a small piece of meat, some bread, or a few vegetables. Sometimes a shell would come driving into the shoppers, splattering bodies along the street. Minutes later, after the wounded were removed, the line would re-form. "There are never any complaints, never any sad and disgruntled faces," Matthews reported. "They gossip and laugh and build themselves little fires, if there is any refuse around, and somehow the time passes." They spent the rest of the war that way, cold and hungry, but proud in their fortitude, their patience, and their survival.

The rebels were still determined to take Madrid. At the end of November they decided to attack the Coruña Road northwest of the city, cutting off the militia holding positions in the mountains of the Sierra de Guadarrama. If successful, Madrid's water and power supplies would be cut and the rebels might yet force it to surrender. Rebel attacks in November and December were contained with heavy losses. But early in January the rebels unleashed a tremendous onslaught, overcoming fierce resistance to push the defenders across the Coruña Road. By January 9 many units of the International Brigade were totally destroyed and the rebel forces sat astride the crucial highway. Once again the Republic counter-attacked, and the armies were locked in their death struggle until January 15, when, exhausted and their ammunition depleted, they broke off the battle and retired behind defensive fortifications. Each side had lost 15,000 men in ten days' fighting; the rebels had penetrated less than ten miles into the Republic's territory, but they did not cut the lifelines to the city. Once again, Madrid had been saved.

The chill winter rains came. Russian air strength finally reached the point where the German bombers could be chased from the skies. But the shellings continued. In the valleys and hills above the city its armed defenders huddled in trenches and behind barbed wire. Within Madrid the hunger, the cold, and the sickness took their toll, but the worst was over. Soon other cities in Europe would know the horrors of terror raids, of street fighting, of fires. But now, Madrid rested. It had survived.

# 8

# *Bitter Battles*

The novelist Arthur Koestler, who covered the war for European newspapers, wrote: "Other wars consist of a succession of battles; this one is a succession of tragedies." Málaga was one of them.

A port city whose population of 100,000 was almost doubled by the influx of refugees from the hill villages above it, Málaga was at the center of a shallow stretch of Republican-held territory along the southern coast. With Madrid beyond the reach of Franco's exhausted army, it was chosen as a target both because it could easily be taken and because it would serve as a good training ground for the Italian troops sent to Spain by Mussolini, who was clamoring for battle. From his Seville headquarters General Queipo de Llano directed 15,000 soldiers of his Army of the South, aided by 5,000 Italians and lavishly equipped with Italian trucks, tanks, and equipment. They launched their attack on January 17, 1937, quickly chewing up villages along the coast, and by the end of the month paused just past Marbella.

Koestler, who arrived in Málaga on January 28, discovered "a city after an earthquake. Darkness, entire streets in ruins, deserted pavements strewn with shells, and a certain smell which I knew from Madrid; fine chalk dust suspended in the air mixed with shell powder and—or is it imagination?—the pungent odor of burned flesh." Italian planes relentlessly bombed the city and gun batteries of the rebel destroyers just outside the harbor pummeled it from the sea. Another reporter called Málaga "a city of the dead," and described the bombings as "a massacre without resistance." The city had no planes and no shelters. The defense was demoralized and disorganized. Truckloads of ammunition were turned back by jurisdictional disputes between union leaders in Almería, up the Valencia road. In Valencia the government remained unconcerned about Málaga's fate, giving it up for lost.

On the road to Marbella militiamen listlessly lounged about, resigned to having to take to the hills when the rebel tanks came. In the mountain passes snaking down to the sea and Málaga, militiamen waited for the enemy, knowing their puny rifles would be useless against the Italian armor. When the rebel offensive started again, on February 3, the defenses crumbled. Panic gripped Málaga, and a few days later a human flood swept along the road out of the dead city, toward Almería and Valencia. Italian troops, on the heights above the escape road, waited, knowing the refugees could be cut off later. Militiamen threw down their rifles, tore off their uniforms, and joined the flood. Their officers crammed into any car they could lay their hands on and fled, too.

Koestler observed the tragic flight of Málaga's poor. "There is a touching conventionality," he wrote, "about the way in which in all great catastrophes—fires, floods, wars—the poor and wretched rescue their bedding before everything else. Next in the hierarchy of earthly treasures comes pots and pans and household crockery. This order of selection of the goods they consider worth saving is perhaps the starkest and most shameless revelation of the permanent misery of the masses of this world. Third on the list comes usually the cage with the canary, the pet cat, or a preposterous mongrel dog; they stand for the sunny side of existence."

On February 8 the Italians marched into Málaga, followed by Queipo's Army of the South and by the Falange extermination squads. People on the death lists were hunted down with such ferocity that the Italians were afraid to turn prisoners over to the Spanish forces. The Italian ambassador had to protest to Franco, who just shrugged and explained that Málaga was a "red" town and that he had no control over the local courts. It was Badajoz all over again; some estimates of the murdered civilians range as high as 4,000 killed in the first week alone. Rebel troops advanced along the road to Almería, stopped the refugee caravan, and released the women and children, but killed the men before their eyes. For the next two weeks the refugee columns were bombed from the air and the sea, German ships taking part in what was a deathly, unopposed target practice for their crews.

And that is how Málaga died.

The deadly exercise in the south ended, the rebels turned once more to the tempting treasure of Madrid. This time they did not attempt a frontal assault but decided to launch an attack southeast of Madrid, aiming for Arganda on the highway to Valencia. Once this vital link with the coast was cut, they would wheel northeast to take the Saragossa highway, isolating Madrid from the rest of loyal Spain. Rains delayed the attack, originally planned for mid-January. The Republic planned an offensive for the same sector and was massing its troops for a drive to cut the rebel lines between Madrid and Toledo, relieving the pressure on the capital.

The Nationalists struck first. On February 5, while the Italian troops were perched at Málaga's edge preparing for their triumphal march into the city, rebel troops made light-

ning raids on Loyalist positions in the Jarama valley. The
next day, supported by German aircraft and artillery, the
main attack began as 40,000 soldiers advanced along a twelve-
mile front. They poured through the Republic's unfortified
lines, gaining La Marañosa, a high peak on which they concentrated their heavy guns, which blasted the Republican
lines and dominated the battlefront. Reinforcements were
rushed from Madrid, and they dug in as heavy rains fell on
the 9th, halting the rebel advance. The next night rebel forces
massed before the Pindoque Bridge on the Jarama River.
Moroccan troops crept across the bridge silently, knifed the
sentries, and then wiped out a whole company of its defenders. When the alarm was finally sounded, electrically
controlled mines set under the bridge were discharged. The
harsh sounds of explosives ripped the air; the bridge quiv-
ered, rose several feet in the air—and then settled right back
on its supports. At dawn Moroccan cavalry poured across it,
threatening to collapse the Republic's lines and break through
to Arganda. The Italians of the Garibaldi Battalion of the
Internationals dug in just above the bridge and, withstanding
the relentless hammering of rebel artillery, swept the bridge
with machine-gun fire for three days, slowing the rebel advance. Russian tanks threw the attackers back across the
bridge, but were themselves driven off by the rebel artillery
firing from La Marañosa. Then the rebels drove deep into
Republican territory; the Moroccan cavalry destroyed a
French battalion of the Internationals; and infantry assaults
on the line of hills in front of Arganda crushed the Polish
battalion of defenders. It looked as though the line would
crumble, but Russian tanks reappeared and Spanish infantry-
men replaced the decimated Poles, and the line held.

The battle of the Pindoque Bridge was repeated at another
key Republican defensive position at San Martín de la Vega,

a few miles south. Once again the Republican mines were poorly placed, and attempts to blow up the bridge only lifted it from its foundations. Once again Moroccan troops slipped across the bridge, slit the throats of the sentries, and prepared the way for a rebel advance. Once again the rebels poured through the breach and captured an important hill from which their guns swept the battle sector.

Furious fighting continued on the 12th. British troops of the International Brigade withstood withering attacks on what they called Suicide Hill, but they held fast, losing two-thirds of their six hundred men and making the rebels believe the area was more strongly defended than it actually was. Bullets flew through the olive groves. One position was lost and recaptured by the defenders five times. The rebels called on increased air support, but as the German planes began their bombing run over the Republic's positions, forty Russian fighter planes appeared and drove them off. By nightfall the defensive lines had held, despite the onslaught of superior rebel forces. When the attack resumed on the 13th, the strengthened defense met furious charges by the Moroccans, who opened wide gaps in the Loyalist lines and destroyed entire units of defenders. But the attacking forces were themselves so badly wrecked that they could not take advantage of the situation; about half of the Moroccan shock troops lay dead or wounded.

On the 14th they tried again. Fighting was bitter, with heavy casualties on both sides. The British were dislodged from their positions on Suicide Hill and fell back to the rear, where the haggard survivors were met by the divisional commander, Colonel Gal, who told them they had to recapture the position: a hole had been opened in the defense and he had no other troops to fill it. The scattered, hungry remnants of three days of brutal front-line fighting pulled themselves together, slowly walking back to the front. Then, perhaps in defiance of the hated Gal, who had ordered a suicidal attack the day before that left many of their comrades dead, they began singing the "Internationale," marching toward the front and attracting stragglers from other units who stopped their retreat in amazement and joined the newly determined Britons. "I look back," recalled an Irish officer. "Beneath the forest of upraised fists, what a strange band! Unshaven, unkempt, bloodstained, grimy. But full of fight again." They fought their way back to regain the lost positions.

The rebel offensive on the 14th was stopped cold. After some initial gains, Russian tanks appeared and sped through the olive groves, their cannon blasting away at the Moroccans, who broke ranks and fled. Time and again the German planes overhead were chased from the skies by Russian fighters. The rebel ranks were blown open, and they switched to the defensive, trying to stem a Republican advance that might crumble their front. A last rebel offensive, ordered by Franco, was snuffed out on the 15th, and the initiative now passed to the Republicans. The Jarama front was assigned to the Madrid sector, unifying the command, and General Miaja now took over.

On the 17th Miaja counter-attacked, hoping to roll the rebels back beyond the Jarama River. His forces advanced swiftly, but the rebels were saved by massive bombing attacks by the German Condor Legion. Trenches were dug and the offensive resumed a week later. This time the Republicans blundered, choosing the most heavily defended part of the rebel front to mount their attack. It was in these battles for Pingarrón, a strategically important rebel stronghold, that the first Americans saw action in the war. Organized as the Abraham Lincoln Battalion, the American volunteers went to their deaths on the 27th under the orders of Gal— now a general—orders that were criminally stupid.

Gal ordered his commanders to take the hill "at all costs," promising air and artillery support. Before the attack could get under way, the trenches of the Lincoln Battalion were placed under constant heavy fire. Ordered to attack anyway, the Lincoln's commander, Robert Merriman, argued that without covering support from troops on his sides, an attack would be suicidal. At noon he was ordered to advance under threat of court martial and the Lincolns went over the top. They were met by an iron curtain of bullets. Few made it more than a few feet beyond the trenches. Merriman was cut down with a shoulder wound as he went over; all of the unit's other officers were killed or wounded within minutes. Then the skies opened and an avalanche of rain fell on the battlefield. The wounded lay in the mud of no-man's-land; the lucky ones squirmed across the dead bodies and into the relative safety of the trenches. Half of the Americans died in that attack, the last Republican attempt to push the rebels back. General Gal was later removed from his command and is reported to have returned to Russia, where, although a loyal Communist, he was shot.

The rains fell and both sides retreated behind their fortifications into wet trenches, huddled under blankets against the fierce cold. About 50,000 men lay dead and wounded; the Foreign Legion, the cream of the Franco armies, was shattered; the Republic's International Brigade was badly mauled. The rebels gained a few miles of land, but the Republic saved its lifeline to Madrid. A standoff: nobody won; both sides lost. The American survivors of the Lincoln Battalion sang a song to the tune of "Red River Valley," recalling the tragic days when death stalked the olive groves:

There's a valley in Spain called Jarama,
It's a place that we all know too well;
For 'tis there that we wasted our manhood,
And most of our old age as well.

Franco still had to capture Madrid, and he now called on the Italian conquerors of Málaga. He massed 50,000 troops along the Saragossa road above Guadalajara, northeast of Madrid. The 30,000 Italians commanded by General Mario Roatta Mancini were lavishly equipped with tanks, armored cars, trucks, and flame throwers and assisted by 20,000 Spanish forces under Moscardó, the hero of the Alcázar, now a general. The plan called for this army to roll down the Madrid road while the rebels in the Jarama valley resumed their offensive, trapping the Republicans in a huge pincer movement that would encircle the capital.

On March 8 the Italians unleashed a dawn artillery barrage and then their armored cars opened a gaping hole in the Republican lines, through which the massed armies of Roatta and Moscardó poured. The overconfident Italians raced ahead, jeering at their Spanish comrades, wondering aloud why Madrid had not been captured after all these months. Then bad weather hit, and snow and sleet storms grounded the Italian planes based in the mountains to the north. But Republican aircraft flying from fields near the front hampered the Italian advance, strafing trucks stalled on the muddy roads. But the breakthrough continued, and Russian and Spanish officers were rushed to Guadalajara to take charge of the defense while their troops were running away from the front. Spanish troops were brought up from Madrid and Internationals moved from the still-quiet Jarama trenches.

The Italian advance continued, and on March 10 the walled

town of Brihuega, just above Guadalajara, fell. The Republican lines stiffened and fierce fighting was taking place. A civil war within a civil war now raged, for directly in front of Mussolini's legions were the Italian exiles of the Garibaldi Battalion, thirsting for revenge against the Fascists who had driven them from their homeland. Their first encounter came in the woods outside Brihuega when they clashed with a Fascist patrol. Hearing Italian spoken on the other side, the Fascist commander demanded to know why they were firing on the Italian troops. "We are Italians of Garibaldi," came the reply, and the outnumbered Fascists surrendered.

On the 11th the attack definitely stalled, and on the following day the weather turned worse and the Republican air attacks increased in intensity. Roatta's troops were now submitted to a barrage of propaganda as loudspeakers were brought up to the front lines and appeals made for desertions. "Go home, you must not die," boomed the loudspeakers. The Italians were told that Mussolini had lied to them, as indeed he had: many of the troops had been told they were going to Ethiopia for occupation duty, and now they were fighting other Italians in the frozen wastes of Spain. Demoralized by the barrage of emotional appeals not to fight their countrymen, knots of Italian soldiers melted across the Republican lines. As the Garibaldis sent Roatta's troops scurrying away in retreat, the Italian general received a wire from Mussolini, who expressed his "unshakable confidence" and asked Roatta to "tell the Legionnaires that I follow their action hourly and their efforts will be crowned with victory." Roatta passed the wire on to his men for inspiration and added that they had nothing to fear from the Garibaldis, since "these men are the same as . . . those whom our Fascist squads thoroughly thrashed on the roads of Italy."

The roads of Spain were a different story, though, and the

Italian lines crumbled before the Russian planes and tanks, the reinforced Republican troops, and the heavy artillery that crushed all attempts to resume the offensive. On March 18 Spanish Republican forces began their push to drive the Italians back. While Roatta was in Franco's headquarters complaining about the failure to launch the promised Jarama attack in support of his troops and screaming for Moroccan reinforcements, a fleet of eighty Russian planes was bombing and strafing his troops. Republican forces stormed Brihuega and the retreating Italians raced away in panic, abandoning their artillery pieces and leaving the highway strewn with their guns, packs, and ammunition—anything that would slow them down. The Republican forces pursued, regaining lost ground, until Franco threw Spanish troops into the breach and a defensive line was organized.

Guadalajara was a clear victory for the Republic, its first after a long, heartbreaking succession of rebel victories. Especially sweet was the rout of the Italians, who suffered high casualties: about 3,000 dead, 6,000 wounded, and another 2,500 taken prisoner. Spaniards on both sides mocked Mussolini's shame; they translated CTV (the Italian initials standing for the "Corps of Volunteers") as *"Cuando Te Vas?"* ("When are you going home?") In Nationalist Spain people sang:

> Guadalajara is not Ethiopia,
> Spaniards, even when Reds are brave;
> Fewer trucks and more guts.

A furious Mussolini vowed that no Italian would be allowed to return home alive unless the shame of Guadalajara was avenged, and complained bitterly that the Spaniards had let his men down. Despite the evidence of Italian intervention paraded by the Republicans in London and at the League of Nations, Britain and France continued their policy of appeasement. Even after the Italian representative on the Non-Intervention Committee declared that his country's troops would not be removed from Spain until Franco won, the French border remained sealed. Franco, whose sole goal since the rebellion was to take Madrid, now reached the inescapable conclusion that the prize was not to be his—yet. Abandoning further efforts to take the capital, he now turned northward, to the isolated Republicans of the provinces along the Bay of Biscay and to the hated Basques.

# 9

# *The Fall of the Basques*

If Madrid lay beyond the rebel grasp, the rich mines and factories of the north offered adequate consolation. Since the fall of San Sebastián, the northern front had been relatively quiet. The Basques busied themselves constructing an "Iron Ring" of fortifications to protect Bilbao, their chief city and an important industrial center. On March 24 an army engineer deserted, taking with him the plans of the half-finished defense line. To defend their leaky Iron Ring, the Basques had about 40,000 troops, very few planes, and far less artillery and munitions than necessary. Ranged against them was an attacking army of 50,000 rebel troops spearheaded by the Navarrese army of Carlists and backed up by the massed might of the planes of the German Condor Legion and Italian artillery and infantry.

Before beginning the attack on March 31, General Mola warned darkly: "I have decided to end the war in the north quickly. Those who are not guilty of assassinations and who surrender their arms will have their lives and property spared. But if surrender is not immediate, I will raze all Vizcaya to the ground." His infantry forces made some quick progress but soon bogged down against tough resistance and bad weather. The planes of the Condor Legion, however, more than fulfilled Mola's threats to destroy the Basques.

On March 31 the German bombers appeared over the sleepy country town of Durango and dropped four tons of bombs on its red roofs. One smashed through a crowded church while the priest was saying mass. Splinters of stained-glass windows mixed with the debris of ruined houses and the twisted bodies of dead civilians as the Germans flew off behind the Nationalist lines, having all but wiped the tiny, peaceful town of Durango from the face of the earth. The Nationalist radio announced that the Republicans had taken advantage of nearby bombings of military targets to burn the churches of Durango. No one believed that the religious Basques, whose priests supported their fight for the Republic, could do this, but some explanation, no matter how outrageous, had to be given for the horrible destruction of an unarmed town.

The brutal bombings went on unopposed. Jay Allen, an American war correspondent who witnessed the bombing of Bilbao, wrote: "They are having a field day, these German and Italian planes. As sportive as porpoises in a squally sea, they leap and dive over the front, over the villages behind the lines, bombing, machine-gunning, strafing down everything that moves. They have nothing to fear."

Then came the tragedy of Guernica.

Guernica is a small town of about 7,000 people, nestled in a valley some fifteen miles from Bilbao. History is about the only thing that separates it from the other small country towns and villages that dot the Basque landscape, for Guernica is the symbol of Basque democracy. In the center of the town stands a gnarled oak tree; in ancient days it was here that the elected leadership of the Basques met to take an oath to respect the rights of the people. In later years when kings ruled a Basque region that became part of Castille, the king or his representative came to take the same oath. The king was but another citizen and all were equal. It was here too that José Antonio Aguirre, president of the autonomous Basque region, swore the ritual oath in October 1936. The little town wore its past proudly but humbly; its people were devout Catholics, farmers and shopkeepers, far removed from the battles that raged at the front.

April 26, 1937, was a market day like any other Monday, and the little town's main square was crowded with the fruit stalls of farmers, and with the sheep and donkeys and the wooden-wheeled ox carts of peasants going to market. Probably few people noticed two planes, mere dots high in the blue afternoon sky. They inspected the town below and then flew off. They were scout planes, harbingers of the Condor Legion's impending attack. At half-past four there was a single peal of the church bell, the warning signal of an air raid. They couldn't be attacking Guernica, but still, people milled about in the square, unsure of what to do. Some, perhaps more frightened than the others, went into the shelters that had been set up since the bombing of Durango. Ten minutes passed, heavy with fear. Then, as if from nowhere, German fighter planes swooped low over the red-tiled rooftops, spitting machine-gun bullets at the crowds below. Within minutes the square was a bloodstained patch of dead bodies, frightened sheep and donkeys, and overturned stalls. Some people raced to the open fields outside the town, but were pursued by the planes speeding just above the treetops, firing away at them. Then the fighters regrouped into a neat formation, turned, and flew off.

The stricken people pulled themselves out of their hiding places to help the wounded and to salvage their possessions. In the distance they heard the heavy drumming sounds of the massive German bombers. Slowly the planes lumbered over

the town and then methodically bombed it, section by section. To their sides and below them, the fighter planes returned, spraying everything that moved on the outskirts of
the burning town. Every twenty minutes waves of German
planes rumbled overhead, dropped their loads of heavy
bombs, and left. For nearly three hours the attack continued
until, in a final spasm of destruction, a last wave of German
planes dropped thousands of fire bombs on the ruins of
Guernica.

That night the only sounds in Guernica were the moans of
the injured, the weeping of the bereaved, the crackling of
flames whose red glow lit the night sky. Seventeen hundred
people, all of them civilians, were dead, and nearly a thousand more wounded. A cry of horror rose up throughout the
world. In Paris the Spanish painter Pablo Picasso covered a
huge canvas of blacks and grays with scenes of death and destruction, and, like the fate of the town that inspired it, his
painting "Guernica" became a symbol of the horror of war.

While the German officers were studying the results of
their experiment in terror-bombing defenseless civilian populations, the wheels of the Nationalist propaganda machine
were set in motion with charges that the "reds" did it themselves. To this day it is not known whether Franco or Mola
definitely ordered the raid, but it is certain that they approved
its result. The Germans, of course, denied their planes were
in the air at all, but Condor Legion commander General Hugo
von Sperrle boasted in 1939 that his planes had done the
job, and in his Nuremberg trial for war crimes, Hermann
Goering lamented: "Guernica had been a testing ground for
the Luftwaffe. It was a pity; but we could not do otherwise,
as we had nowhere to try out our machines."

On the ground, rebel forces steadily pushed the Basque
defenders back over the trench-pocked hilltops toward Bilbao.

The Republic tried to help the Basques, although the Valencia government was torn by internal dissension that erupted in bloody riots in Barcelona. Aircraft was the Basques' most urgent need, but the only way the Republic could safely send planes to Bilbao was over French territory, with refueling stops at French airports. A few attempts at sending planes this way ended with Non-Intervention Committee observers seeing through the scheme and sending the planes back to Catalonia. Once, fifteen planes landed at Toulouse airport in military formation, all claiming to have lost their way and requesting permission to refuel and fly back to Bilbao. After being warned that if such incidents happened again the planes would be confiscated, the Republic sent ten planes directly to Bilbao in a desperate gamble that they would make it through the mountains and the German- and Italian-dominated skies. Seven did, but by the beginning of June all had been shot down. And no more Loyalist planes came.

On June 3 General Mola was on his way from Burgos to Franco's headquarters at Salamanca. With the exquisite irony of fate so typical of the war, Mola's plane crashed on Brujula Hill outside Burgos, and the burning hulk of the general's plane smoldered on the very place that saw hundreds upon hundreds of ordinary citizens shot in cold blood and buried on that very hill during the months of terror that followed the rebellion. The general and his victims now shared the same tragic hill. Few people mourned the organizer of the rebellion, and on June 11, under the new command of General Fidel Dávila, the Army of the North renewed its attack on the thin ring of Basques before Bilbao.

By the afternoon of the 12th they were at the final perimeter of Bilbao's defense, the Iron Ring, and by the 15th this final barrier was breached and the road to Bilbao lay open. In the city itself the government supervised the evacuation of civilians to the comparative safety of Santander. Shells poured on Bilbao and enemy planes strafed refugees on the roads out of the city. A fleet of fishing boats carried nearly half its population to safety. Earlier, in May, several thousand Basque children had been sent from the war zone to live in England, where the appearance of even a single light civilian plane in the sky was enough to send the younger children scurrying for shelter, screaming *"Bombas, bombas!"*

With Bilbao certain to fall, the Basque government left also, leaving the defense of the city in the hands of a junta led by Jesús María de Leizaola, who decided the city would be surrendered without unnecessary bloodshed and in a civilized way. His actions were typical of the Basque approach— dignified and realistic. He ordered the bridges blown up and military factories sabotaged; political prisoners were released without reprisals and the historic church and the university buildings protected. On the morning of June 19 the last militiamen left the empty city, and by late afternoon the red and gold flag of the Nationalists waved above the Basque capital. Basque freedom was ended and the use of the Basque language forbidden. Within weeks German experts were inspecting the iron mills and factories of the Bilbao industrial complex, restoring them to war production.

The only way the Republic could avert the loss of its remaining northern provinces was to go on the offensive elsewhere, thus forcing the rebels to draw troops and equipment away from the north. The Republican high command chose to try to roll back the rebel lines west of Madrid. An army of 50,000 was assembled just above the rebel-held town of Brunete, with orders to drive due south and relieve the pressure on Madrid. If successful, another attack would strike north, trapping the rebel armies in a wide pincer movement that would finally free Madrid. This first major Republican offensive of the war started on July 6, and it achieved an immediate breakthrough. Temporarily by-passing rebel strong points, the Republican army swept through to Brunete, strongly supported by Russian tanks and aircraft, now with Spanish crews. Rebel reinforcements were rushed to the shattered front and managed to stop the advance in fierce fighting. By the 13th the offensive had ended with the Republic in possession of Brunete and a swatch of land about five miles deep and seven miles wide.

On the 18th the rebels unleashed a vicious counter-attack, backed by the planes of the German Condor Legion, and masses of equipment pulled back from the Army of the North. Under the broiling Castilian sun the armies were locked in bloody battle. Losses were enormous on both sides, and once again the Internationals bore the brunt of the casualities. Among those killed was Oliver Law, commander of the Lincoln Battalion and the first black American ever to command predominately white American forces in a war. The rebel superiority in the skies turned the tide. The German planes kept up a constant barrage of the Republic's troops. "It was simply overwhelming," wrote Republican General Vicente Rojo. "Night and day the planes fell upon us with a frequency and a potency unknown until that time." And an American survivor wrote that the earth "heaved and rocked and swayed and roared and smoked, and the bombs kept coming down, and every time you heard the whistle and scream you knew there was a shaft pointing at the small of your back and the bomb would hit you right there and blow you to a million pieces."

By the end of July the Nationalists had won back most of their losses, and although the battle ended in a stalemate, it was a clear disaster for the Republicans, who had lost 25,000 men and much irreplaceable equipment. The Nationalists might have been able to follow up the demoralized Loyalist army with a renewed assault on Madrid, but Franco cautiously returned to the northern campaign.

The rebel strategy was to pick off the northern provinces, piece by piece. First the Basques fell; now the Army of the North turned to adjoining Santander, weakly defended by the poorly equipped remnants of the Basque army that had lost Bilbao. On August 14 the rebels started their push, taking one hill after another until they had advanced to the Bay of Biscay. In the lead were three Italian divisions out to redeem the reputation they had left on the road to Guadalajara. With resistance useless, the Basque defenders of Santander surrendered. Thousands of people fled in fishing boats as the Fifth Column rioted in support of the invaders.

The Basques chose to negotiate a surrender to the Italians, knowing full well the hatred the Nationalists had for them. The agreement removed the Basques from the war: they agreed to surrender their arms in return for solemn Italian guarantees that there would be no persecutions, that the Basques would not be forced to fight in Franco's army, and that Basque politicians and civil servants—the prime group marked for reprisals and murder by the rebels—would be allowed to leave the country. On August 27 two small English boats, the *Seven Seas Spray* and the *Bobie,* entered the harbor at Santoña and the waiting Basques started to board them. Then Italian soldiers drove up the dock, pointed machine guns at the lines of waiting Basques, and ordered the ships emptied. An angry Franco had countermanded the Italians' agreement with the Basques, and the next morning the ship captains saw their former passengers marched out of the city to the inevitable drumhead trials and murder. The rebels, who claimed to be fighting a Catholic crusade against the godless "reds," killed sixteen Basque priests and drove more than four hundred others into exile. Just as the Republic persecuted the Church because it had cut itself off from the people, the Nationalists persecuted the Basque Church because it was loyal to the cause of the Basque people.

All that remained of the Republic in the north was a pocket in Asturias, the mining province. Since July 1936 the capital, Oviedo, had been in the hands of the rebel Colonel Antonio Aranda, who had won it by a brilliant deception. Immobilized by a continuing siege of loyal miners and militia, Aranda held out, but now he was reinforced and the rebel Army of the North moved to take the province. Hampered by the lack of air support, which was concentrated in Aragon, the scene of another Republican offensive designed to help the beleaguered northern fighters, the rebels struggled against a determined defense for six weeks. Then, weary and running low on ammunition, the defense broke, and by October 21 Asturias was in Nationalist hands. The Republic no longer existed in the north.

The fighting in Aragon, like the Brunete offensive, aimed not only at relieving pressure on the north but on making a strategic breakthrough against a weakly held Nationalist front. On August 24, just days before the fall of Santander, the Republicans attacked around Saragossa, hoping to surround it and break the rebel front in the northeast. The attack was stopped cold on its northern front, but in the southern sector, around the key towns of Belchite and Quinto, there were some initial gains. As in the Brunete campaign, the Loyalist forces broke through the rebel lines and then were held up by faulty communications among their units and by the inability to keep up with their advancing tanks. The attack was stalled by the inability to take heavily fortified towns, one of which, the key crossroads town of Belchite, was besieged by Spanish troops. After it was almost devastated by artillery barrages, Spanish and American troops clawed their way through fierce resistance, battling the Nationalist defenders in a week-long struggle that carried them from house to house and block to block. Ernest Hemingway, covering the battle as a reporter, wrote that the fighting was "of the sort you never know whether to classfy as hysterical or the ultimate in bravery." When Belchite finally fell to the Republicans, it was a ruined hulk, with eight-foot-high piles of corpses and flames licking at the remnants of what once was a favorite resort area.

The struggle to take Quinto and Belchite so drained the Republic's limited resources that it could not press its brief victory. Fighting continued throughout October, but the Aragon offensive ended in stalemate. It never became a serious enough threat to delay the rebels' northern campaigns, and while the Republic clung to some of the territory it had won at such great cost, it was left in a weakened and exhausted position. By the fall of 1937 the Republic had been reduced to a stretch of territory in eastern and south-central Spain somewhat in the shape of an enormous fist, with its apex at Madrid and its wrist in the Levant attached to the wide forearm of Catalonia. All of the rest of Spain was in Franco's hands.

The international situation facing the Republic deteriorated throughout 1937 as well. Britain held firm to its appeasement policy in the face of the evidence of massive Italian and German intervention that made a mockery of the Non-Intervention Committee. The British, desperate for an accommodation with Mussolini, signed an Anglo-Italian "gentlemen's agreement" in January to stabilize the Mediterranean situation, but the ink was barely dry before the Italian dictator landed 4,000 additional men in Spain and attacked Málaga.

In the spring dozens of vessels were attacked by Italian submarines in the Mediterranean, and in late May the entire situation boiled over with a Republican air attack on the German battleship *Deutschland* in the harbor of Ibiza. The Germans retaliated by assembling a small fleet which bombarded the undefended coastal city of Almería, killing twenty-four, wounding well over a hundred, and destroying much of the port. In June the Germans charged that another of their ships had been fired upon and, with Italy, withdrew from the Non-Intervention Committee's coastal patrols. The collapse of the sea patrols led the French to retaliate by opening their border unofficially, allowing arms to be smuggled to the Republic. Had this been done earlier, the Basques might have been saved. Now, it had little effect on the Republic's situation.

Throughout the summer Italian piracy in the Mediterranean increased. The Russians, a dozen of whose freighters were now rusting at the bottom of the Mediterranean Sea, cut back their aid shipments from six boatloads in July to only one freighter in all of September and October, the months of the Aragon offensive. Stalin was beginning to reconsider his stake in Spain; the British and French were no closer to realizing the threat of the Hitler-Mussolini alliance, and they reacted with total indifference to the new war between Japan and China that was threatening Russia's vast Asian frontier. Franco was beginning to look like a winner, and the risks of helping the Republicans increased daily.

As the tempo of the Italian sea raids increased the British were finally moved to action. Early in September, after two British ships had been bombed and another sunk—the last of a long series of harassments faced by her ships—Britain called an emergency international conference at Nyon, Switzerland, to take action against further outrages at sea.

On September 14, with Germany and Italy absent, diplomats of nine countries agreed to act to protect merchant shipping. Britain and France would send warships to the Mediterranean to destroy any ship of any country that interfered with the free flow of seaborne trade. The British then proceeded to throw away whatever gains they made by this firmness. Incredibly, they invited Italy to join the Nyon pact's sea patrols—in effect, to chase themselves. The Italian Foreign Minister, Count Ciano, chuckled that he was a "pirate now turned policeman."

The plight of the Republic was becoming grim, and the inaction of the world's democracies was responsible for it. "Bilbao, Santander, the Asturias were all defended by as brave men as ever went into battle," raged David Lloyd George, Britain's Prime Minister during the First World War, in Commons. "But they had no guns. Who is responsible for that? Non-intervention. Who is responsible for keeping non-intervention alive? His Majesty's Government. If democracy is defeated in this battle, if Fascism is triumphant, His Majesty's Government can claim victory for themselves."

KEYSTONE

*Manuel Azaña (left) and General Gonzalo Queipo de Llano (right) in June 1931. Azaña became Prime Minister of the Republic in October of that year. Queipo de Llano joined the rebellion against the government in 1936.*

KEYSTONE

*A poster of the Popular Front seen everywhere in Madrid.*

KEYSTONE

*Republican militiawomen parade in the arena in Madrid.*

KEYSTONE

*The entry of General Francisco Franco (center) and General Emilio Mola (right of Franco) into Burgos, rebel headquarters, in 1936.*

KEYSTONE

*The ruins of the Alcázar in Toledo.*

*Pablo Picasso's famous painting "Guernica" expresses the torment and devastation of the bombing of that Basque town in early 1937.*

COLLECTION, THE MUSEUM OF MODERN ART, NEW YORK
ON EXTENDED LOAN FROM THE ARTIST

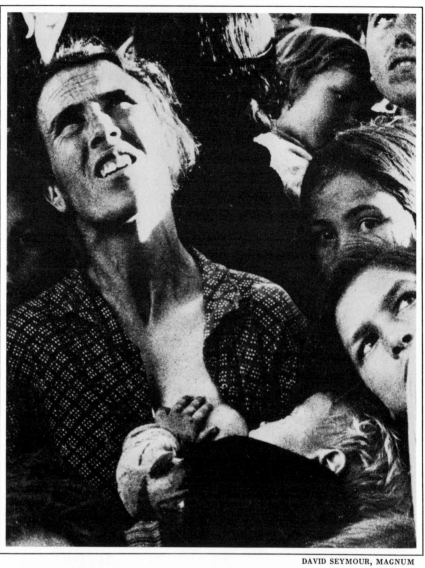

DAVID SEYMOUR, MAGNUM

*The anguish of the Spanish peasants was captured in this photo made in Estremadura in 1936.*

DAVID SEYMOUR, MAGNUM

*General Miaja, commander of Madrid's Loyalist defenders.*

KEYSTONE

*Government militia in the Casa de Campo during the battle
for Madrid.*

ROBERT CAPA, MAGNUM

*Foreign volunteers give the Loyalist salute as they prepare to leave Spain toward the end of the war.*

KEYSTONE

*The Nationalist victory parade in Madrid, 1939. Franco, in the honor stand, receives the salute of his troops.*

ROBERT CAPA, MAGNUM

*Refugees en route to France as the war ends.*

KEYSTONE

*A meeting between Hitler (far left) and Franco in the south of France in October of 1940.*

# 10

# Behind the Lines–
# Nationalist Spain

Rebel-held Spain, meaning about two-thirds of the country
by late 1937, was a military dictatorship that presented an
uneasy mixture of traditional authoritarianism and some of
the Fascist trappings of its German and Italian allies. Its supreme leader, "El Caudillo," was General Francisco Franco
y Bahamonde, the forty-four-year-old, five-foot-three-inch
former desert fighter whose photos were plastered on every
window, shop front, and wall in the country. Sometimes they
showed him standing, somewhat paunchy, in battle dress; but
most of the time he was portrayed in close-up, his balding
head covered by the tasseled cap of the Foreign Legion. In
only a few months he had moved from being reluctant co-
conspirator of the generals planning the rebellion to its chief.

In its first days the rebellion was led by a makeshift junta
run by Mola but nominally headed by an elderly moderate,
General Miguel Cabanellas. Early in August, with the Army
of Africa crossing the Strait, Franco and Queipo de Llano,
who ruled Andalusia as if it were his personal fief, were
added to the junta. But feeling grew that the rebels should
come under a unified command since wars are not won by
committees, and General Alfredo Kindelán, a Monarchist
who believed Franco would restore the king, pressed the junta

to name him commander in chief. This was readily agreed
to and late in September, while Franco was making his
triumphal visit to the Alcázar, his supporters rammed a
decree through the reluctant junta naming him chief of state
as well. On October 1, 1936, he took office in Burgos, promising to protect workers and peasants and to do away with
voting. "Fran-co, Fran-co," the crowds of Nationalist Burgos
chanted. He adopted the Monarchist colors for the flag of
Nationalist Spain, having unfurled the red and gold banner
earlier in Seville on a hot day in August, surrounded by
Queipo, priests, and other army men. "Here it is! It is yours!
They wanted to rob us of it!" Franco screamed at the huge
crowd in a city that had never cared for the monarchy and
couldn't quite understand why Franco was pressing the king's
flag so energetically to his lips. But such outbursts were rare
for this cool, contained military man who proved himself
a master politician and came to pulverize all opposition to his
personal power.

Perhaps the single outstanding characteristic of Nationalist Spain was what became known as the "White Terror"—
the systematic destruction of liberal views. "The enemy,"
wrote American reporter Edmond Taylor, "was a complex
molecule of a spiritual poison called communism for con-
venience; but liberalism was the most deadly individual element in it and the most hated. Introduced into the human
organism, this poison acted like a germ virus; not only incurable but infectious. . . . [Liberals] had to be shot in a
human way because they were incurable and might infect
others." It was this kind of thinking, this division of Spaniards into those who were saved and those who had to be
shot because of their liberal beliefs, that led rebel-held Spain
into a reign of terror that continued long after the war itself
came to an end.

At first, the White Terror was relatively unorganized: bands of Falangists, Guardias, and right-wing political functionaries killing off Popular Front supporters (or personal enemies) under the benevolent gaze of the military. The most famous victim of these killings was Spain's leading poet, Federico García Lorca, who was torn from his hiding place with friends who had right-wing connections and murdered by a rival faction. "Oh that the crime was in Granada," lamented his friend the poet Antonio Machado. "Let all know it. Poor Granada. In his Granada!" In the area around Burgos the slaughter was so extensive that as late as August 1937 the provincial health officer had to order the immediate burial "of any dead bodies found abandoned outside the town."

Majorca, today a popular tourist paradise, was the scene of some of the worst mass killings. In August 1936 it was occupied by Italians, who remained for the duration of the war, using it as an air and sea base. Civil power was turned over to a red-bearded Fascist Black Shirt, Arconovaldo Bonaccorsi, who called himself General Count Aldo Rossi. This madman raced around the island in a sports car followed by assorted clerics and gunmen, and presided over horrible convulsions of murder. The Catholic writer Georges Bernanos watched truckload after truckload of innocent peasants driven away to their slaughter and estimated 3,000 killings in just seven months. If Majorca was an extreme situation, it was not totally untypical. Mola was heard to admit: "A year ago I would have trembled to sign a death sentence. Now I sign more than ten a day with an easy conscience." Most of the victims of the Terror were dragged from prison cells in the dead of night, or were shot down in the fields falling into graves they had been forced to dig, or were found on the roadside and buried without identification, for people feared to admit knowing them. No one knows how many there were, but the historian Gabriel Jackson estimates some 200,000 people were murdered in the Nationalist zone in the less than three years the war lasted.

After more than a year of uncontrolled killing, Franco moved not to end it but to regularize the murders. In January 1938 he appointed a seventy-five-year-old retired general, Severiano Martínez Anido, as Minister of Public Order. Years before, in the early 1920's, this same general had presided over an official terror campaign against Barcelona Anarchists and leftists. Now, he pursued his new assignment with such thoroughness that even the German ambassador was moved to suggest to Franco that the killings be moderated. The excuse given for the killings was that some 40 percent of the people in the "liberated" areas were against the regime and had to be cowed into submission by terror. There was ample evidence of resistance to Franco in the occasional guerrilla raids on troops in the rear, attacks on bridges and military installations, and the presence of large guerrilla bands in Asturias and in the southwest. But the Germans, and even some leaders of the Falange, feared that continuation of the Terror would make it impossible to govern the country after the war. Not only did Franco ignore his friends' advice, but he set up a special documentary section to obtain proof of war crimes on the Republican side so that the score could be evened later on.

Few people in Nationalist Spain dared speak out for humane values. One who did was the aged, world-famous philosopher Miguel de Unamuno, rector of the ancient University of Salamanca. On October 12, 1936, at a special university ceremony for the "Festival of the Spanish Race," an important holiday, he met his exact antithesis, General José Millán Astray, the founder of the Spanish Foreign Legion, whose empty left sleeve, black-patched right eye, and deep scar across his cheek all testified to his sacrifices in the colonial wars in Morocco.

Their confrontation—the thoughtful philosopher and the organizer of the Legion whose song spoke of death as a bride —was a classic meeting of two strands of Spain's past, the sun-filled world of humanity and the dark underside of death-obsessed souls. In the solemn Ceremonial Hall of the university the general poured forth a torrent of abuse against the half of Spain he said were criminals: the treasonous supporters of the Republic, along with the evil Basques and Catalans who were "cancers in the body of the nation." Millán screamed the Legion's battle cry, *Viva la Muerte!* "Long Live Death!" Blue-shirted Falangists in the audience gave the stiff-armed Fascist salute to a portrait of Franco, hanging, out of place, on the wall of the university chamber. "Fran-co, Fran-co, Fran-co," they shouted while Unamuno sat watching with contempt.

When the seventy-three-year-old philosopher rose, he immediately stated, "You all know me and are aware that I am unable to remain silent . . . to be silent is to lie, for silence can be interpreted as acquiescence." He called Millán "a symbol of death," who "is wont to seek ominous relief in seeing mutilation around him." When Millán's supporters broke into his talk, Unamuno said: "This is the temple of the intellect and I am its High Priest. It is you who are profaning its sacred precincts. . . . You will win, but you will not convince. You will win, because you possess more than enough brute force, but you will not convince, because to convince means to persuade. And in order to persuade you would need what you lack—reason and right in the struggle. I consider it futile to exhort you to think of Spain. I have finished."

In the silence that followed, the great philosopher was led

from the stage, supported on one arm by none other than the wife of General Franco. He was placed under house arrest. In ill health and harassed by thoughts of what was happening to his beloved country, he died on December 31, 1936.

Rebel Spain was marked by the extraordinary growth of the Falange—from less than 70,000 in July 1936 to almost a million by the end of the year. The Falange was not only a key element in the White Terror and the repressions, it also became the savior of countless leftists who used the blue shirt as a life preserver. Correspondents observed people tearing up their Communist and Anarchist party cards as they crossed the threshhold of Falangist recruiting offices. These "new shirts," as they were called, were responding to Falange posters that assured them "the past means nothing to us," as well as to other posters that warned: "With us or against us? There is no middle course. Falange awaits you." Other "new shirts" were former members of the CEDA, whose leaders, including Gil Robles, had to spend the war in Portugal or in hiding for fear of Falangist gunmen. A German observer reported that "the members of the Falangist militia have no real aims and ideas; rather they seem to be young people for whom it is good sport to play with firearms and round up Communists and Socialists."

The organization lost its charismatic leader, José Antonio, who was trapped in his Alicante prison cell when the rebellion burst. Tried for treason, he was executed on November 20, 1936, and soon was canonized as a Nationalist saint. Franco decreed the day of his execution a day of national mourning; streets, military units, and special projects were named for him; and rebel Spain embarked on a permanent campaign of hero-worship, deftly organized by Franco, who knew how to turn the death of a potential rival into a political victory for himself.

The secret of Franco's political success, both during and after the civil war, was his remarkable ability to play one power bloc off against another and to continually adjust the delicate political balance of the country so that all groups would be too weak to challenge him and too content to want to do so. In the spring of 1937 he moved to defang the two main political forces in Spain, the Falangists and the Carlists, who were constantly quarreling with each other. Both represented potential threats to Franco's power. The Falange might become a tool of the Germans, and the Carlists, fanatical in their monarchism, had dared to set up a military school of their own, which Franco suppressed.

Persuaded by his most powerful adviser, his brother-in-law Ramón Serrano Suñer, to end the political vacuum in Nationalist Spain by creating a state party, Franco fused the rival Falangists and Carlists into a single organization on April 19, 1937. Falange leaders were thrown into jail on trumped-up charges and Franco himself became the leader of the new party, called FET for short. Franco himself never referred to it as anything other than The Movement. Symbols of the Falange and Carlist groups were absorbed into the party, and this shotgun marriage forced Falangists to don the hated red berets of the Carlists, while the reluctant Monarchists had to wear the despised blue shirt of the Falange. The party program was a hodgepodge of Fascist doctrine and vaguely Monarchist ideals and glorified the Caudillo:

> As author of the Historical Era in which Spain achieves the possibility of realizing her historical destiny, and with it the goals of the Movement, the *Jefe* [Chief] assumes absolute authority in its utmost plenitude. The *Jefe* is responsible before God and before History.

Since it was a movement more than a political party, everyone was a member—army officers, civil servants, and officials at all levels, as well as ordinary citizens. It became a vehicle for national unity and army control, and fused workers and employers into syndicates, or unions, that were used to enforce state control over the economy and to regulate workers for the benefit of the industrialists and large landowners who supported the Franco dictatorship. The Movement itself soon deteriorated into a sort of employment agency, dispensing government jobs but exercising little real control, which remained in the hands of the military.

The major lines of Franco's dictatorship were modeled after the regimes of Hitler and Mussolini. When Germany and Italy formally recognized the Nationalists as the legal government of Spain on November 18, 1936, Franco effusively stated that "this moment marks the peak of life in the world." The following July he promised in a speech that his Movement would "follow the structure of totalitarian regimes such as Italy and Germany . . . but will have specifically Spanish characteristics." Public decrees and even private letters in Nationalist Spain were dated Year I or Year II in honor of the military rebellion. Most of the country was administered by government offices in Burgos, the dry Castilian city that reminded one American reporter of an Arizona frontier town. Military headquarters were based in the medieval atmosphere of Salamanca, and Franco, who spent much time in both places, also had a mobile headquarters that was moved near the active fronts.

The military was revered. Officers ran the country until the first regular Cabinet took office in January 1938, and they dominated that, and succeeding, Cabinets. A uniform, whether army or militia, was a passport to respect, and civilian men were often mocked with remarks such as "men who don't wear uniforms should wear skirts." Educated young men were made temporary second lieutenants to fill the need for more junior officers, but the toll among them was so great that a popular saying was "temporary lieutenant, permanent corpse." Most of the million men in the army and the militia were draftees.

Next to Franco, the most famous general in the Nationalist zone was the erratic, unpredictable Queipo de Llano, whose nightly radio broadcasts, mixing off-color jokes, crackpot philosophy, personal attacks on the Republic's leaders, and a heavy dose of gossip, were the most popular form of entertainment. Queipo may have acted the clown but he earned the nickname "the social general" by genuine social reforms that improved the lot of the peasants around Seville, although his reforms were counter-balanced by the real repressions he led against workers. His ambitions were quashed by Franco, who smothered the semi-independent Seville regime with the power of the centralized totalitarian state.

In general, material living conditions were better in the Nationalist zone. While Madrid suffered famine and in the later stages of the war Republican cities were hit by terrible food shortages, food was fairly plentiful in the rebel-held territory, since it included Spain's major wheat-producing areas. Coal and fuel were plentiful, thanks to foreign aid, and the economy hummed along fairly smoothly. In addition to German and Italian supplies and American oil bought on credit, trade with England was brisk.

But the restrictions on the lives of ordinary citizens were considerable. Rigid censorship was enforced: unfriendly foreign journalists were expelled, the state took full control over Spanish newspapers, and books of leftist "tendencies" were destroyed "as a matter of public health." A progressive labor law was not regularly enforced and workers were forbidden to form unions other than the state-run syndicates, or to strike. Land reform consisted in the return of Republican-confiscated land to their former owners. Freedom of religion was abolished, and the Church restored to its former power. Franco, who had never been especially religious, now backed the Church with the zeal of a convert. When he heard that the petrified hand of Saint Teresa of Avila had been discovered among the booty taken in Málaga, he ordered it sent to him, and the grisly relic spent the rest of the war on his bedside table.

Franco's restoration of the Church's privileges, combined with the Republic's massacre of priests in the early days of the rebellion, won the Nationalists the support of the Vatican. Pope Pius XI's first public statement regarding the war, in September 1936, condemned the Republic for its "truly satanic hatred of God," but stopped short of endorsing Franco. The Spanish hierarchy backed the general vigorously; in July all but two of Spain's bishops published a collective letter claiming that the army had protected the Church and forestalled a Communist Spain. Parish priests fulminated against atheists, "reds," liberals, Jews, and Masons. The Masons, a fraternal order that had been the seat of anti-clerical liberals, along with outright leftists, were prime victims of the repression. After the conquest of the Catholic Basques, which resulted in the persecution of the Basque clergy, the Vatican officially recognized the Franco government.

While Franco welcomed the Church's support, his relations with his two main allies, the Germans and the Italians, were wary. Both would have preferred Spain to be under the leadership of a less stubborn, more pliant individual. As the Nationalists slowly ground away at the Republic in an apparently never-ending province-by-province campaign, Italy's patience wore thin and Mussolini occasionally threatened to withdraw his troops. He was in too deep, however; Italy's prestige was on the line, and he never did it.

Spaniards disliked the boastful Italian Fascists in their midst more than the Germans who were fewer, thus less visible, and who went about their business in a workmanlike way. A popular story in rebel Spain was that of a barber who asked an Italian soldier why he was there. "To capture Santander and Bilbao and fight communism," his customer replied. Next in the barber's chair was a German pilot whom the barber also asked, "Why did you come here?" "I came to get shaved," was the reply. But like other foreign troops who are sent to fight in another country by their governments, Condor Legion pilots often laughed that "we are fighting on the wrong side."

The Germans found Franco a tough negotiator and won the mining concessions and mineral rights they coveted by playing on the Nationalists' desperate need for the services of the Condor Legion and for uninterrupted shipments of supplies from Germany. Joint German-Spanish trading companies were set up to handle imports and exports, and these handled deliveries to Germany of the industries of Bilbao and the wealthy lodes of Spanish and Moroccan ores. Although Franco successfully stalled the broader German demands for much of the duration of the war, he eventually had to consent to sweeping economic dependence on Germany and to follow much of the advice given by German army officers who were settled into offices at his headquarters. Just as the Republic was forced to excessive reliance on its Russian supporters, so, too, was Nationalist Spain overly dependent on Germany and Italy.

The triple alliance of Spain, Germany, and Italy pervaded the daily life of the country. "Portraits of the three dictators appear on postcards," Harold Callender reported to *The New York Times*. "Every hotel this traveller has seen in Rebel

Spain displays German, Italian, and Insurgent flags together. Mussolini's face, framed in a tin hat, glowers from the walls. Hitler's visage and book are shown in every town. The only foreign papers and magazines sold are German and Italian and one pro-Fascist London paper."

# 11

# *Behind the Lines—*
# *Republican Spain*

If Nationalist Spain suffered the iron rule of dictatorship, many people thought Republican Spain's problems were caused by too much democracy. The revolutionary chaos that followed the army rebellion left Loyalist Spain in ferment, but the government was powerless, a centralized army nonexistent, and the Republic's supporters split into mutually antagonistic factions that were often at each other's throats. By the end of 1936 the revolutionary thrust had spent itself. The people, after the first flush of revolutionary enthusiasm, were coming to grips with the real problems of survival and the Valencia government of Largo Caballero was gradually regaining control.

The first step was to end the indiscriminate terror. Except for Madrid, which was on the front line, and where reprisals against Fifth Columnists were still going on, the persecution of the middle classes and of political dissidents was largely ended. Nationalist terror continued until long after the end of the war, but the Republic's excesses lasted for only a few months—long enough, however, for more than 20,000 persons to have been killed. Justice was now dispensed by a system of "people's courts" that tried criminals as well as political offenders, and reforms were made in the prisons.

The second step was to bring the revolution in the country-side under control. The government legitimized land take-overs by peasants, and by 1938 about a third of all the farm-land in the southern part of Republican Spain was officially turned over to the peasantry. At the same time, however, the Republic moved ruthlessly against the Anarchist collectives that blanketed Catalonia and Aragon. It disbanded the revolu-tionary committees that ran local villages and redistributed communal land and farm equipment among individual peas-ants and former tenants. By the summer of 1937 the troops of the Communist general Enrique Lister were ruthlessly wiping out the effects of the revolution in Aragon.

Although they were welcomed in those villages that had had collectivization imposed upon them by the Anarchist columns of Durruti in the wild days of the summer of 1936, even those places that had enthusiastically embraced the Anarchist system were forced to abandon it, including collec-tives that were freely organized before the July rebellion. This led to anger and discontent, and in some places the fight against the collectives had to be abandoned until after harvest time.

The third major step Largo Caballero took to restore power to the central government was the creation of a Popular Army to replace the hodgepodge of union and party militias. The ultra-democracy of the militias was hampering the war effort: even minor decisions were voted on. Militiamen took brief vacations from the front at will, and they abandoned the most elementary military procedures, for example, launch-ing night attacks with exuberant shouts of *"Viva, viva"* that alerted the enemy instead of surprising him.

The new Popular Army came to life step by step in a series of decrees that enlarged the government's control over the militias, instituted a draft, and reorganized fighting units into mixed brigades that combined military functions such as infantry, artillery, and transport under a single brigade command. The Communist Fifth Regiment, the strongest and most respected of all the Loyalist forces, set an example by disbanding and was absorbed into the new army. But it took time before the new system functioned, and the Anarchists' columns pouted in their trenches, refusing to give up their own unit names and flags, and other militia units had to be patiently taught that saluting officers was neither undemocratic nor harmful.

The new army was dependent on Russia for its equipment, and much of its leadership was drawn from officers who had served in the Communist militia. Professional officers who served in the pre-1936 army were politically suspect and most were assigned to positions in the rear. Russian military advisers played a major role in setting strategy, often overruling government officials. The Popular Army took the Russian five-pointed red star as its insignia, and the Popular Front's clenched fist salute was introduced. It also adopted the Russian system of political commissars for each unit.

The commissar, wrote an American reporter, Vincent Sheean, was "guide, philosopher, and friend to the men in his unit; he is responsible for their political education, their morale, their spirit; he has to explain the government's actions to them, and see to it that they have a very clear idea of why they are fighting." The commissar was responsible for far more than political indoctrination or maintaining a good fighting spirit. He was charged with ensuring that the troops got proper food and hygiene, and he served as a kind of ombudsman to handle soldiers' gripes. An important function in an army drawn from a largely illiterate population was teaching reading and writing—some 75,000 troops learned how to read in 1937 alone.

The commissar system helped mold a more effective army, but it also served to increase Communist control over the armed forces. The growth of the Communist Party in the Republic, like that of the Falange in Nationalist Spain, was a remarkable, war-induced phenomenon. At the time of the rebellion the party numbered about 30,000 members, but by mid-1937 it was claiming over 400,000 members, with hundreds of thousands of other Spaniards enrolled in its youth division and in Communist-front organizations controlled by the party. Part of the reason for this extraordinary growth was the Communists' superior discipline and efficiency that attracted many people fed up with the excesses of the Anarchists and the inability of the old-line Republicans and Socialists to govern effectively.

The prestige of Soviet Russia was another factor in the growth of the party. Russia was the only country to supply arms and advisers in quantity; it was Russian planes that helped save Madrid and Russian tanks that spearheaded the victory at Guadalajara. Russian revolutionary films played in all the movie houses, and main squares were decorated with large photos of Stalin, Marx, and Lenin. A grateful people turned to the Russians as their saviors from Franco, and their task was made easier by the new-found moderation of the party. Not willing to antagonize potential allies in England and France, the Communists were all for putting the brakes on the revolution in Spain. The Communists' headquarters in Barcelona was plastered with signs that read: "Respect the property of the small peasant," and "Respect the property of the small industrialist," thus winning them middle-class support. Stalin, who had just forced collectivization on Russian farmers at a cost of several million lives, joined this campaign in a December 1936 letter to Largo. Russia's dictator suggested, as comrade to comrade, that Largo respect private property, encourage parliamentary democracy, and cooperate with Azaña and the Republican moderates.

As the Communists grew in strength and self-confidence, they began to move aggressively against their enemies on the left—the Anarchists and their allies of the POUM, a small extremist party in Catalonia. Anarchist militiamen refused to disband and were hoarding weapons and munitions needed more urgently by the army at the front, and the government kept arms and troops back in Valencia against the possibility of a revolt. Many Anarchists believed that after Franco was beaten, the Republic's guns would be turned on them and they viewed parliamentary democracy, like fascism, as a bourgeois invention to defeat direct control of the workers.

The Communist campaign against these "uncontrollables," as they were called, was initially launched by the Cheka, the unofficial Communist secret police force that dominated the government's secret police. The Cheka operated independent of the control of the Minister of the Interior, who had to tolerate the Cheka's separate prisons and separate investigations, admitting, "Well, we have received aid from Russia and have to permit certain actions which we do not like." Anarchists charged that eighty of their comrades had been murdered by the Communist secret police in the spring of 1937.

In March the Catalan government decreed the end of the workers' patrols that had replaced local police forces in much of the region and ordered all political organizations to surrender their weapons. The conflict raged all spring, with the government and the centralizers, aided powerfully by the Communists, ranged against the die-hard Anarchists and their POUM allies who refused to give up their arms.

By the end of April tensions had mounted to the point

where a civil war within the civil war seemed likely. Anarchist and Communist gunmen were shooting each other; two prominent Anarchists were assassinated, the government moved loyal carabineers to take over control of the border from the militia, and the Catalan government finally gave dissidents forty-eight hours to hand over their guns. The Anarchist newspaper *Solidaridad Obrera* thundered: "The proletariat in arms is the guarantee of the revolution. To try to disarm the people is to place oneself on the other side of the barricades. Let no one permit himself to be disarmed!"

On May 3 Catalan officials, determined to take over full control of public services in the region, went to the central telephone exchange in Barcelona with several truckloads of Assault Guards and demanded that the Anarchists turn the building over to the government. Shots erupted in answer. Within hours the hidden arms were brought out, barricades erected, and the streets of Barcelona given over to pitched battles between workers and police. By nightfall chaos ruled and the government controlled only a small portion of the city. Smaller risings occurred elsewhere in the province and Anarchist and POUM militiamen began to march on Barcelona from the front in Aragon.

Neither side really wanted full-scale warfare while the Republic was fighting for its life against Franco, whose offensive against the Basques was then reaching its height. Only weeks before, Franco had solved his own problems of political factionalism by forcing the Falange and the monarchists to merge, and loyal Republicans thought they could solve their political problems in a more democratic way. Negotiations were started to end the fighting, and leaders of the CNT rushed to cool things off. The columns marching on Barcelona were asked to return to the front, and the two leading Anarchists in the Largo Cabinet, Federica Montseny and Juan García Oliver, pleaded for a truce. García said: "It is necessary to put an end to this fratricidal struggle. Let each remain in his position without trying to use the truce in order to conquer the others."

A shaky truce was arrived at, but it was constantly broken as one or another of the many armed groups in Barcelona fired on its enemies. CNT leaders begged their followers to go back to work, while the POUM and the Anarchist extremists called for a fight to the finish. In Valencia, Largo was slow to move against the rebellion of the Left. He distrusted the Communists, believing they had provoked the rising, and feared they would use it as an excuse for seizing power. Finally, he was forced to send several thousand Assault Guards from Valencia to enforce the truce on May 7. By that time, deserted by their leaders, the workers who had risen spontaneously in defense of their revolutionary aspirations had melted away from the barricades and returned to their jobs. By May 9 life was back to normal—more or less. The extreme Left had been defeated; the private stores of arms were finally seized by the government; the Anarchist militia was disbanded, and the Popular Army placed in control of the Aragon front.

But the cost to the Republic was enormous, and not just in the estimated 1,500 casualties of the week's fighting. The failure of the May revolt left large numbers of Catalan Anarchists embittered; it deprived the CNT leadership of much of their popular support; and it placed the government in a compromised position of having to use arms against its people. Because so many Catalans were demoralized and disheartened by the loss of what they considered to be their revolutionary gains, enthusiasm for the war effort eroded, and the indifference of so many people made itself felt in lowered production and decreased efficiency. Finally, the crushing of their only viable opposition strengthened the Communists and gave them a stronger hold on the Republic.

The Communists pressed their advantage against their weakened opponents, and hundreds of POUMists and militant Anarchists were arrested by the Cheka. The POUMists were a special target since they were Communists who refused to accept the mandates of Stalin. Some of their leadership had been followers of Leon Trotsky, Stalin's rival for power in Russia, and now the worst accusation that might be made by a Communist was to call someone a Trotskyite, or a follower of the exiled leader. Largo resisted Communist demands to eliminate the POUM, and this was just the latest of a long series of confrontations that led the Communists to resign from the Cabinet on May 15, forcing President Azaña to name a new government.

The Communists—and many loyal Republicans—considered Largo incompetent. They blamed him for the fall of Málaga, criticized his refusal to organize guerrilla units to harass the rebel rear, and rejected his scheme to pull troops from the vital Madrid front to start an offensive in the southwest. Largo did have his faults, but he was an honest patriot, a man of the Left who, for all his violent rhetoric, was committed to extending Spanish democracy. He successfully resisted the Communists' persistent demands, backed by Stalin, that the Socialist Party merge with them, and he once threw the Russian ambassador out of his office, screaming after him: "Get out! Get out! You will have to learn, Señor Ambassador, that although we Spaniards are very poor and need help from abroad very much, we are too proud to let a foreign ambassador attempt to impose his will on the Head of the Government of Spain!" Alarmed by the growth of Communist power in the army, and especially among the commissars, he issued an order on April 17 that no one could serve as commissar without his personal approval.

President Azaña knew that reappointing Largo might mean the end of vitally needed Russian supplies, so he turned instead to Finance Minister Juan Negrín, a Socialist allied with Largo's moderate rival, Indalecio Prieto. Negrín was a study in contrasts with the aged Largo, who had taught himself to read while a young adult and who had been a worker and trade-union leader for a half-century. Negrín was a doctor, a professor of physiology at the University of Madrid who headed the committee that had supervised the building of University City, now a bullet-pocked battlefield on the Madrid front. Although the Communists backed him, their support was based on the fact that his sophisticated personality would make a good impression abroad, and his technical expertise and efficient management would improve the war effort.

Negrín was a political realist who knew the Republic's existence depended upon Russian aid and who continued Largo's attempts to limit Communist penetration of the army and the government. He, too, rejected proposals to merge the Communist and Socialist parties, backed Prieto's efforts to limit Communist control of the army, and tried to be independent of Russian advisers. When they called him "comrade," he corrected them, insisting on being addressed as Señor Prime Minister, and he told the Russian economic adviser not to meddle in Spain's internal affairs or, he warned, "there is the door." He flew to Paris to try to convince the French to change their mistaken policy and to aid the Republic, in part because Russian shipments were slowing down, but also because he wanted to reduce his reliance on the Communists. "The western democracies," Prieto lamented after the war, "fearful of communism, did not realize that this movement grew in Spain as a result of their own lack of assistance."

In matters related to the war effort and to increased military efficiency, Negrín found the Communists able allies. As the military picture worsened and pessimism took hold, they were almost his only supporters in pressing the fight against the rebels. His biggest clash with them came over the activities of the Cheka. In June the Communists produced forged letters purporting to show that the POUM was spying for the Franco forces. Espionage did exist, and the Republic had found a number of spy rings, including one that reached into General Miaja's staff in Madrid, but although the charges against the POUMists were phony, the party was banned and its high officials arrested by the Communist police.

The POUM leader, Andrés Nin, disappeared, and an angry Negrín called in the Communist Party leader to demand information. As a "Where is Nin?" campaign mounted, the Communists disclaimed any knowledge of his whereabouts. Negrín was tempted to break relations with Russia then and there, but with no other country in the world willing to ship arms to the Republic and Franco's forces in possession of two-thirds of the country, he had to swallow his pride and give up his inquiries. Actually, Nin was a prisoner of the Communists in a torture cell in Alcalá de Henares, where attempts were made to get him to sign a Russian purge-style confession implicating others. Despite the most awful tortures, Nin held out and refused to sign anything. Finally, his captors murdered him after staging a fake liberation by German-speaking Communists who dropped identifying documents to make it look like a Gestapo rescue attempt. The real truth only came out after the war.

Negrín moved to overcome the scandal caused by the Nin

disappearance; he dashed the Communists' hopes for a Moscow-style show trial of POUM leaders, and instead they received fair trials that brought "not guilty" verdicts on the charge of treason. Negrín strengthened the government's control over the secret police and over the prison and court systems, liberalizing them and cutting Communist influence. In August he authorized Catholic Church services in Republican Spain and in the army, and in October he rejected Communist demands for new elections for the Cortes. Negrín's running struggle to preserve his independence against the encroachments of the Communists took place against a backdrop of the indifference of the democracies, charges of being a Communist dupe, and the continuing challenge of trying to improve the living conditions of the Spanish people while fighting a war against an enemy determined to extinguish all opposition.

Life in Republican Spain was difficult. Food shortages were commonplace, and Madrid was especially hard hit as the long siege dragged on. It became the chic thing for foreign writers and celebrities to visit Madrid, and the Hotel Florida on the Gran Vía became the temporary home of writer Ernest Hemingway, famous war correspondents and playwrights, and even adventurous actors in search of some free publicity, like matinee idol Errol Flynn. Materials of all kinds were scarce, and that led to lowered production of both civilian goods and war equipment. The endless flow of refugees from the war zones was an enormous strain on the Republic's ability to feed, clothe, and house them properly. They slept in bullrings, subway stations, and parks, or were crammed into whatever housing could be found for them.

As early as January 1937 a Quaker relief group estimated 25,000 homeless children in Barcelona, and by year's end the city had to absorb an additional 800,000 refugees.

Food rations were at about half the normal pre-war diet, and the long lines that formed in front of food shops in the early days of the siege of Madrid now became a regular feature of life all over Republican Spain. An American relief worker described a factory in Murcia that might have held 500 people in crowded conditions serving as home for 9,000 refugees from Málaga. Children under six were given four prunes for lunch, sometimes with bread, which helps to explain the growing number of deaths from malnutrition. "The children are pitifully thin and ragged," one observer reported, "and they have the brown, withered look that comes with prolonged hunger."

Despite the war and its pinched resources, the Republic tried to cope with these desperate conditions. Compulsory inoculations helped prevent the spread of disease; child welfare centers were organized, government spending on education was five times the pre-war level, and credits were granted farmers to buy seed and equipment. The tradition of nonrevolutionary reform started by the Republic was thus continued even under wartime conditions. There was much about Republican Spain to disturb foreign liberals—the growth of Communist influence, press censorship, and repression— but the delicate scales of justice were weighted on its side, for it still enjoyed a degree of legitimacy and popularity not found in Nationalist Spain, and its struggle to preserve its independence from both the Russians and the Fascist-supported rebels compelled admiration and sympathy. The Loyalists still represented "the last great cause."

# 12
# *Breakthrough*

As 1937 drew to a close the Two Spains had over a million men in arms. The rebels had 600,000 troops plus the Italians and Germans fighting alongside them, outnumbering the Republican army. They had far more planes, artillery, and tanks than the Loyalists did. During the course of the year they had added giant chunks of Republican territory— Málaga and the area around it in February, the entire northern region by October. The battles around Madrid—the Jarama and Guadalajara campaigns—had ended in stalemate, as had the Republic's diversionary offensives around Brunete and Belchite. And the Republic lost men, too, at least 50,000 dead and 200,000 wounded in that long and bloody year.

The war was going badly for the Republic; it was being drained of land and of men. Intelligence reports now indicated a massive build-up for a rebel offensive against Madrid —a replay of the Guadalajara strategy of cutting the capital off from the northeast, but this time with greater firepower against a weaker Republican defense. The Republican general staff decided to beat Franco to the punch with an offensive of its own that would force him to postpone the attack on Madrid and pull troops away to meet it. They chose as their target Teruel, a lightly defended hill town of perhaps 15,000 people in Aragon that was the tip of a finger-shaped slice of rebel territory surrounded on three sides by the Republic.

On the morning of December 15, 1937, with blizzard winds of fifty miles per hour driving a curtain of snow in front of them, 40,000 Republican troops advanced on Teruel. By evening, temperatures had plunged to well below zero and snow still fell on roads covered by a layer of solid ice. Teruel was encircled, and on December 21 the Popular Army entered the town fighting their way inch by inch among the ice-covered streets and alleys. On the 23rd, with the rebel garrison holed up in the southern end of the town, Franco called off his planned offensive on Madrid and rushed troops to retake Teruel.

This was exactly what the Republic hoped he would do, for by this time it was clear that Franco's guiding policy was to try to recapture every foot of lost ground. For reasons of prestige, he was willing to call off or delay more important strategic plans in favor of rescuing some less vital position, as in the relief of Toledo's Alcazar that may have cost him Madrid, and again at Teruel. His German and Italian advisers told Franco to forget about Teruel and go after the big prize—Madrid. But the stubborn little general wouldn't listen. Franco was gambling that instead of a crushing blow which would end the war quickly, he could count on German and Italian arms to win a long, drawn-out war of attrition that would slowly bleed the Republic to death. It was the technique of the bullfight—lead the enemy on; stab him with the pic and the *banderillas,* force him to waste his energies in fruitless charges and attacks, and then, when he is exhausted, finish him off with a deft slash of the sword, leaving him to die in the blood-soaked sand.

While the Republicans laid siege to the rebel garrison, fresh Nationalist troops advanced toward Teruel and Condor

Legion planes smashed Loyalist positions. On New Year's eve the rebels captured a peak overlooking the town, La Muela de Teruel, Teruel's Tooth. The fighting was all but suspended for the next four days as a bitter blizzard paralyzed the battlefield. The sub-zero cold now claimed as many casualties as the fighting; frostbite was common, and medical units on both sides had to amputate frozen limbs in hastily improvised field stations. Trucks supplying the troops snaked their way along the ice-slicked roads, treacherous even in good weather, and many skidded off into the deep ravines. When truck engines froze over, stalling the convoys behind them, movable parts were stripped from their bodies, and they were thrown over the hillsides to clear the way.

Within the city, heavy fighting continued with the dwindling rebel defenders finally giving up on January 7. The Nationalists branded the rebel commander, Colonel Rey d'Harcourt, a traitor for this, but the truth is that he had no alternative; if anything, he should have surrendered his troops, three-quarters of whom died or were wounded in the fighting, and the 2,000 civilians they protected, much earlier. Now the situation was completely reversed; the rebels occupied much of the high ground above Teruel, and the Republicans manned a besieged garrison within the town.

While the frozen armies confronted each other in the snow and ice, Franco's Italian allies were driven frantic by the apparently endless delay in launching the rebel offensive, and Mussolini warned that Italy could not be "tied up in a war which drags on forever." Finally, in late January, Franco's forces began a powerful counter-attack. German artillery gunners poured such a heavy bombardment on Republican positions that it was estimated that "there was no five-yard square that had not received its shell." By February 21, 1938, the Nationalists had cut off the Republican defenders and were back in Teruel, where they found 10,000 dead soldiers of the Popular Army and took 14,500 prisoners.

Franco now finally abandoned his plans to take Madrid. He had massed a powerful army on the Teruel front, only a hundred miles from the sea, and, rather than pull it back to another front, decided to reinforce it for a blow that would slice the Republic in half. Along a fifty-mile front stretching from Teruel to Huesca, near the French border, the Nationalists placed more than 150,000 troops, including the crack units of the Foreign Legion, the Moors, and the Italians. They were supported by nearly 1,000 airplanes, including the most advanced models from Germany; over 300 tanks, and abundant artillery, trucks, and armored cars. Facing this awesome display of military power, the most powerful build-up of the war, was a weak Republican force of about 35,000 men still recovering from the slaughterhouse of Teruel, with perhaps 60 planes and 60 tanks and fewer heavy guns.

At dawn on the morning of March 9 the rebel artillery opened up all along the line of attack, the heavy shells churning the hardened ground into a deathly moonscape. The sky above was black with rebel aircraft, bombing and strafing the Republican troops, who were caught by surprise. Then hundreds of rebel tanks rumbled across no-man's-land, firing as they went. Within hours the Republican lines had crumbled. The motorized attack moved so swiftly that Republican reinforcements hastily rushed from positions in the rear found that the rebels had got to their assigned defensive positions first. Within a week the rebels had overrun the scenes of earlier hard-fought battles, towns such as Quinto and Belchite, and had surrounded and isolated entire Loyalist units. The Republican army was all but crushed; rebel casualities were light, less than 1 percent of their armies.

In the northern sector the rebels penetrated into Catalonia

for the first time in the war, capturing the key city of Lérida early in April. In the south, the Italians and the choice Galician Corps were advancing in the desolate wastelands below the Ebro River. Fighter-bombers pounded the defenders; a survivor of the Lincoln Battalion's last-ditch stand described the way "they came in slow, slipping from side to side to cut speed. They first make a run and then come in with a shower of small bombs on the position. They repeat this over and over." The shell-shocked remnants of the Internationals and the Popular Army, harried by the enemy fighters, fled in disorder, pressing on for fear of being cut off behind the rebel lines by the tanks speeding along on their flanks. Each time a unit dug in to make a stand against the rebels, it found itself outflanked by the mobile attackers and had to resume the retreat. The shallow hills and parched fields were full of tiny bands of Republican soldiers making their slow, painful way toward the safety of the Ebro River. The defeat had turned into a rout. The Republican army in the southern sector of the rebel advance no longer existed; only a handful of battle-weary men wandering in hopes of escaping the sure death of capture by the rebels. Of the 550 Americans who were caught up in the meat grinder of the Nationalist offensive, only about 100 were left to tell their sad tale of death and destruction.

On April 15 Franco's forces reached the sea. The Republic was split in two. Above a thirty-mile strip of rebel-held seacoast below the Ebro was Catalonia; below it, the Republican central zone, a jagged circle with Madrid, cut off from Barcelona, on one side, and Valencia, just under the rebel lines, at the other.

Throughout much of the victorious Aragon offensive, Mussolini was enthusiastically bombing Barcelona and other coastal cities to break the Republic's will to fight. Ciano, referring to an eyewitness, though probably exaggerated, description of one such raid on Barcelona, wrote: "I have never read a document so realistically horrifying. And yet there were only nine S.79s and the whole raid only lasted a minute and a half. Large buildings demolished, traffic interrupted, panic on the verge of madness, and 500 dead and 1,500 wounded. It is a good lesson for the future." The bombings were held up for a while to force Franco to use the Italian infantry in combat, but resumed in mid-March with a raid on Barcelona that the German ambassador described as "terrible." Seventeen raids over a three-day period killed and wounded more than 3,000 civilians. Franco finally asked that the raids be ended because of the backlash caused by shocked public opinion in France and England. Mussolini agreed, merely shifting the attacks to smaller towns along the coast and chortling that "he was delighted that the Italians should be horrifying the world with their aggressiveness for a change, instead of charming it by their skill at playing the guitar."

Mussolini's brief moment of joy—his troops as part of the Nationalist drive to the sea—was soon dispelled by one of those military decisions of Franco's that drove the German and Italian advisers up the walls with frustration. Instead of marching northward, into Catalonia and toward Barcelona, since October 1937 the Republic's capital, he wheeled his troops southward, toward Valencia. Franco thought that Catalonia would be too strongly defended, whereas attacking to the south would widen the gap between the two halfs of Republican Spain, making each weaker. But capturing Barcelona would mean the end of the war, while marching southward would only continue the slow bleeding of Spain.

Once again, the Republic showed its extraordinary ability to bounce back from disaster. The rebel attack, launched from the Teruel region across the line reaching to the sea, began well enough, but then the heavens opened and a fierce storm left the roads impassable. That attack ended on April 27, and others in the weeks that followed made slow progress, slamming head-on into strong Republican defenses that stopped the rebels well above Valencia.

The rebel victories, the bombings of Barcelona, and the heroic resistance of the Republic led to sharply increased sympathy for the Loyalists. In mid-March of 1938, Mussolini's bombers were killing civilians in Barcelona, Franco's troops were pushing the Republic's front lines back in Aragon, and Hitler's army had just marched into neighboring Austria, focibly merging that country into Germany and leading many Frenchmen to conclude that war was just around the corner. A new Popular Front government in Paris finally opened the border with Spain and arms shipments began pouring through. The Russians, who had cut their aid because of the effectiveness of the Nationalist-Italian blockade and because of the need to fortify their Asian frontiers against Japan, now sent three hundred planes to France, which gladly sent them on to Catalonia.

Hitler turned from swallowing Austria to menacing Czechoslovakia, and as alarm at German aggression spread in the world's capitals, support for the Republic grew. In Washington an effort was mounted to end the embargo and send military aid to the Republic. Many people agreed with Henry L. Stimson, a former Secretary of State known for his conservative views, who wrote—after the effort failed—"If this Loyalist Government is overthrown, it is evident now that its defeat will be solely due to the fact that it had been deprived of its right to buy from us and other friendly nations the munitions necessary for its defense. I cannot believe that our government or our country would wish to assume such a responsibility." Intense pro-Republic lobbying and public sympathy for the Loyalists led the State Department to recommend an end to the embargo. But America's ambassador to England, Joseph P. Kennedy, protested any change in policy, and a counter-lobbying effort convinced President Roosevelt to keep the embargo.

Roosevelt was influenced by England, whose foreign policy set the pace for America. The English Prime Minister, Neville Chamberlain, wanted the Spanish business ended, preferably with a Franco victory, and he was sure that he could arrange for Hitler's ambitions to be satisfied short of a European war. Although the January 1937 agreement with Italy was broken by Mussolini before the ink was dry, he signed still another pact in April, once again calling for the maintenance of the status quo in the Mediterranean and for the Italians to leave Spain *after* a Nationalist victory. Britain remained blind to the Fascist threat even though submarine attacks on its ships in the Mediterranean actually increased after the signing of the agreement, which Winston Churchill called "a complete triumph for Mussolini." The British were also pressing a plan for the withdrawal of foreign volunteers in Spain, not including the Moroccan troops in the rebel armies. After the ineffective fashion of the Non-Intervention Committee, the plan went through interminable drafts and was still being talked to death in the summer of 1938.

In the Nationalist zone morale was dropping after the false hopes that the success of the Aragon offensive would end the war quickly. The White Terror was alienating many Nationalists. When 4,000 Spaniards fled the fighting near their mountain village in June, crossing the border to France, only 168 asked to be sent to the Nationalist zone; all the rest asked to be sent to Catalonia. The Italian terror raids against Barcelona angered many Spanish Nationalists. Street fighting broke out between Italian and Spanish troops behind the lines, and the pro-Falangist General Yagüe had to be disciplined by Franco after he made a speech praising the bravery of Loyalist soldiers and calling the Germans and Italians "beasts of prey." The massive offensive in the spring had almost depleted rebel supplies, and Franco was forced to make major economic concessions to the Germans, giving them new mining rights, in order to get more arms.

Within the Republican zone there was mounting pessimism and war-weariness. The failure of the Teruel offensive and the rebel successes that split the Republic in two led many to conclude that Franco would win. The leading pessimist was Prieto, the Minister of Defense, whose gloom was so deep that Negrín had to dismiss him early in April and take over the ministry himself, vowing to continue the war come what may. Negrín became the embodiment of resistance, a leader in constant motion, always with the troops at the front or visiting factories and villages in the rear, infusing all with his energetic optimism. On May 1, 1938, Negrín declared his government's Thirteen Points, the war aims of the Republic. These pledged the political and economic independence of Spain, a free election to decide the country's future, no reprisals against political enemies, civil rights for all citizens, and other general aims for a free, better post-war Spain.

The Thirteen Points were designed to win foreign support for the Republic as well as to inspire loyal citizens with a set of humane principles for which they could continue their sacrifices. But they were also a basis for negotiating peace with Franco. Negrín did not expect the Nationalists to accept the Thirteen Points, many of which were hateful to them, but if they agreed to a few key ones, such as an end to foreign intervention, free elections, and no reprisals, a negotiated peace could be concluded. Negrín made some contacts with the German embassy in Paris and once flew to Switzerland, pretending to attend a medical conference, yet actually meeting with the Nationalist Duke of Alba, but these and other efforts were in vain. Franco's policy was unconditional surrender and he refused all peace overtures.

Negrín did not think that the Republic could win the war, especially when Britain again pressured the French into closing the border in June. "Not a day passed until almost the end," wrote his Foreign Minister, Julio Alvarez del Vayo, "when we did not have fresh reasons to hope that the western democracies would come to their senses and restore our rights to buy from them. And always our hopes proved illusory." Negrín pinned his hopes for Spain's salvation on the inevitable general European war between Russia, England, and France on one side and Germany and Italy on the other. Such a war would end German aid to Franco and bring the democracies into the civil war. Until then, the Republic must hold out.

But in order to hold out, the Republic first had to demonstrate that it could pull together its shattered army and that it was capable of carrying the fight to the enemy. Early in July Loyalist soldiers began intensive training in river crossing, stocks of arms were piled up, and a regrouped army of 100,000 men massed along the Catalonian side of the Ebro River. The Republic was planning a massive attack on the rear of Franco's army, which was facing west, bogged down in its attempt to take Valencia. It was to be a last, desperate gamble.

On the night of July 24, 1938, the advance guard of Internationals and Popular Army troops silently crept into small boats to cross the Ebro. When one soldier asked the leader of the Lincoln Battalion, Milton Wolff, how they would get back if the offensive failed, Wolff replied, "We weren't coming back." The crossing was successful, the lightly manned rebel rear guard was wiped out, and the next morning the Republican army swept across bridges thrown across the river. By the end of the first day they had driven a large wedge almost ten miles long and six miles deep in the rebel lines. They expanded their attack and within two weeks occupied five hundred square miles on a front that was ninety miles long. But by that time the Nationalists had swung all their firepower around to meet the advance, and the Republican troops tried desperately to hold their gains and avoid being thrown back across the river.

Franco's strategy was similar to that of Teruel—he met the Republic's challenge on grounds of their choosing and persisted in a head-on counter-attack to tear away their gains. His German and Italian advisers were disgusted. They urged that the rebels leave the Republicans in their pocket on the Ebro, swing around the exposed enemy flanks, and drive into Catalonia above the Loyalist lines. This would strike at the Republic's heartland while cutting off the Loyalist army from the rear. A furious Mussolini told Ciano: "Put on record in your diary that today, August 29, I prophesy the defeat of Franco. Either the man doesn't know how to make war or he doesn't want to. The Reds are fighters—Franco is not."

Throughout August the Nationalists hammered away at the thin Republican defenses, all the while carrying on an enormous build-up of artillery and airplanes behind the lines. The initial Republican offensive had been marked by heavy fighting and high casualties, but the battle now was unprecedented for its ferocity. The rebels dropped 10,000 bombs on the troops clinging to hillsides under the harsh, relentless sun. By mid-August half the Americans who crossed the Ebro were dead and wounded. The Lincolns found themselves in "a scene of a blackened, war-torn, and destroyed land. Dead burros lay everywhere. Bodies were everywhere, too. They stank. Everything was burnt to a crisp." There was no place to dig trenches in the harsh rocky mountains, so they piled rocks and spent shells as fortifications, which were all but useless in the face of artillery barrages that went on without a break for seven hours at a stretch. "All day, hour after hour, they kept it up," Alvah Bessie recalled. "They covered our parapets and every inch of the back side of the hill. They wanted, by the sheer weight of their steel, to blow us off that hill."

The battle of the Ebro became a huge slaughterhouse as the massive rebel barrages poured an unending stream of steel on the defenders. In one sector of the front their artillery averaged 14,000 shells a day for 114 days. Rebel aircraft completely dominated the skies. The question was no longer whether the Republicans could hold on, but whether they would be able to retreat across the Ebro in time to avoid total destruction. The campaign, which began under the intense rays of the July sun, ended in mid-November, with the first light sprays of falling snow. On November 18 the rebels were back on the banks of the Ebro.

The Republic's army was chewed up in the meat grinder of the battle of the Ebro: 20,000 lay dead on the jagged hills, 20,000 were taken prisoner, and nearly 60,000 were wounded. Rebel casualties were much lighter, 4,000 dead and 30,000 wounded; and they were able to trade more mining concessions to the Germans to replenish their spent munitions. But the Republican army was all but wiped out. It lacked the manpower to make good its losses; its ranks were already full of men either older or younger than the draftees of the rebel army; and their immense losses—of guns, munitions, artillery, and aircraft—were irreplaceable.

# 13

# The Death of the Republic

The Republic did not lose the war when it lost the battle of the Ebro, nor did it lose it on the other battlefields of Spain. The war was lost elsewhere—in Munich, Germany, on September 29, 1938.

On that day the prime ministers of Britain and France capitulated to Hitler's demands for annexation of part of Czechoslovakia. The Czechs, deserted by their allies as the Spanish Republic had been in 1936, became the victims of Britain's fantasy that Hitler might yet be satisfied short of war. Russia's reaction to Munich was predictable; Stalin finally decided that the western democracies would never form a defensive alliance with Russia. He interpreted their policy as a design to egg Hitler on to expand eastward at Russia's expense, in the hope that the two countries would eventually destroy each other. Stalin concluded from this that if the West would not ally with him against Hitler, he would ally with Hitler against the West. Spain was written off as lost, and after Munich the Republic was quietly abandoned by its only source of military supplies.

Munich came as the hills above the Ebro still resounded with the thunder of Franco's ferocious, drawn-out counterattack. Negrín continued his vain efforts to reach a compromise peace. On September 21, while the Czech crisis was at its height, Negrín went to the League of Nations to announce that he was disbanding the International Brigades and invited the League to supervise the withdrawal of foreigners from Republican Spain. Negrín felt that if the Internationals left, an obstacle to peace would be removed. Further, they were no longer militarily useful to the Republic; their ranks had been shot to pieces, and most of the units of the International Brigades were now made up of Spanish soldiers and officers.

On October 2 Negrín broadcast a plea to Spaniards to stop killing each other and come to some kind of reasonable compromise. The British suggested a Munich-type international conference to settle the Spanish question, a clear invitation to Franco to win a negotiated peace in his favor, but Franco held firm to his terms of unconditional surrender.

On November 15, in Barcelona, the International Brigades held their farewell parade. Huge throngs cheered the war-weary departing troops. Spaniards pushed through crowds to shake their hands, kiss their cheeks, and to place garlands in their hair. The eloquent La Pasionaria recalled the proud days of Madrid's resistance and told the soldiers: "You can go proudly. You are history. You are legend. You are the heroic example of democracy's solidarity and universality. We shall not forget you, and when the olive tree of peace puts forth its leaves again, mingled with the laurels of the Spanish Republic's victory—come back!" Few eyes were dry that day in Barcelona, a Barcelona weary with war, hungry, overcrowded with refugees, and stricken with fear as the shrill sounds of battle along the Ebro crept closer.

Franco now prepared to capitalize on his victory at the Ebro with an onslaught that would bring Catalonia to its knees. New arms were arriving daily from Germany, and he still had the best of the Italian troops that remained after Mussolini pulled out 10,000 men as his gesture of good will to the British. The Republican army on the other side of the Ebro was a broken hulk, short of guns and ammunition. On December 23, after brushing aside a papal appeal for a Christmas truce, the Nationalists crossed the river into Catalonia.

After slow progress in the face of spirited resistance, the superiority of the rebel forces turned the tide and the Nationalist and Italian armies raced up the coast. By January 14, 1939, they were in Tarragona, halfway to Barcelona. The Republic again tried the tactic of launching an attack far beyond the lines of a rebel offensive, hoping to force Franco to respond. But this time the plan failed, and while the Republic's Andalusia offensive gained ground, it never became a serious threat. As the Nationalists moved closer to Barcelona, where more than a million refugees had fled, panic struck the city, which was bombed daily. The rebels now faced almost no resistance. The road leading to Barcelona was jammed with rapidly advancing Nationalist forces; the roads leading out of the city, toward France, were jammed with half a million people in desperate flight. On January 26 the rebel troops marched into the undefended capital, the tramp of their boots against the cobblestoned streets the only sound in the silent ghost city.

The one thought on everyone's mind, it seemed, was to escape to France. The story of the Spanish Civil War is, in part, the story of the ordinary people of Spain fleeing guns and war and death, pushing the tiny carts loaded with their few earthly possessions and trudging along wasted roadways in the hope of saving their lives. They fled burning Irún that way, in the summer of 1936. They poured out of humble villages to escape Franco's Army of Africa in the first year of the war, sleeping on Madrid's streets under German bombing attacks and the chill wind and rain. Clinging to their little bundles of humble household goods, they streamed out of Málaga in 1937. In the winter of 1938 they ran ahead of the invaders to the streets of Barcelona. Now the Spanish masses were marching again, struggling along the roads leading to France or climbing the snow-covered passes of the Pyrenees.

By February 10 all Catalonia was in Nationalist hands, and some 200,000 civilians and 250,000 disarmed Republican soldiers were just across the border in emergency camps in France, tasting the bitter, tear-stained experience of exile and separation. Conditions there were terrible. The French were reluctant hosts—unwilling to help the Republic survive during the war, they preferred not to have to cope with 450,000 refugees. The swiftness of the rebel advance meant that the French were totally unprepared for the massive influx of terror-stricken homeless people. Some of the camps were nothing more than open stretches of sand dunes surrounded by barbed wire and armed guards. Food was short, medicine lacking, and sanitation dreadful. Many of the wounded, weakened by flight, died. Even if the French had flooded the camps with food and medicines, tragic sufferings would have occurred, but there is evidence that the French government hoped, by a policy of neglect, to force its unwelcome guests to voluntarily return to Nationalist Spain. Conditions later improved somewhat: eventually, about 150,000 of the refugees were resettled in Latin America; some in England, Belgium, and Russia; 50,000 returned home to face imprisonment and, often, death; and the rest remained in France.

During the flight to the frontier, the Cortes held its last meeting in the damp dungeons of an old medieval castle

at Figueras, on the road to France, on February 1, 1939. It
endorsed Negrín's new peace terms; the Thirteen Points had
shrunk to three basic conditions that, if agreed to by the
rebels, would lead to the surrender of the Republic. Negrín
insisted on guarantees of Spain's independence, free elections to decide the form of the new government, and guarantees against reprisals. The last point was the crucial one; if
Franco would guarantee the safety of the Republic's supporters and officials, the war could end immediately. Negrín
knew that the war was lost when Catalonia fell, but he could
not conclude peace unless the safety of Loyalists was ensured.

Franco's answer came in the form of a Nationalist Law
of Political Responsibilities, decreed on February 9. The law
made most of Republican Spain liable to fines and imprisonment for up to fifteen years for such "crimes" as belonging
to a Popular Front party, supporting the Republican government in any way, being a Freemason, or engaging in "grave
passivity," that is, not actively supporting the rebels. The
law was retroactive to October 1934, two years before the
rebellion, and it meant punishment for anyone who had
stood by the legal, freely elected government of Spain at
the time of the July 1936 rebellion. Merely to have served in
the Republican army—and nearly a million men were under
arms at one time or another—was to be open to charges of
killing Nationalists and a death sentence as accessory to murder or "armed rebellion." Foreign observers were amazed at
the brutal harshness of the law, and Republican leaders knew
that unconditional surrender now meant mass murder of
their followers.

Negrín felt he had no choice but to continue the struggle
until Franco could be persuaded to grant more humane surrender terms. The Republic still held Madrid and a third of
Spain; it still had an army of 400,000 men, although the

Catalonia offensive had destroyed nearly all its equipment and the cream of its troops. But the army was low on ammunition and the civilian population was war-weary and half-starved. President Azaña and other major Republican figures remained in France, giving up the war as hopeless. Britain and France said they would recognize the Nationalists if Franco would not take vengeance on his enemies. All Franco would say on this score was that the Nationalists would only punish criminals, "reprisals being alien to the Nationalist movement." That was good enough for Chamberlain, and the British and French granted formal recognition to the Nationalists as the legal Spanish government. As for a negotiated peace, Franco stated: "The Nationalists have won, the Republicans must therefore surrender without conditions."

Negrín now tried to rally the remnants of his army. After a meeting with top generals in Valencia, he told Alvarez del Vayo: "The rebels don't need motorized divisions against people with such a morale. A few bicycles would be enough to break up the front." The two men drove to Madrid to canvass the parties and unions to see if they would agree to continue the fight. On the way, Alvarez del Vayo wrote, "We passed by houses which had recently been whitewashed, less out of a desire for cleanliness than in order to efface the anti-Fascist signs which in the early days of the war were to be seen on all sides." In Madrid, Negrín found that the Communists were willing to continue to resist, but the Madrid army commander, Colonel Segismundo Casado, complained about conditions among the civilian population, lack of military equipment, and the arrogance of the Communists. Negrín promised supplies and promoted Casado to the rank of general. He distributed other promotions, reshuffled some military commanders, got a pledge from Miaja to continue to resist, and faced down the leaders of the

Communist Party who were insisting that any peace settlement be based on his three points. Negrín, who now only
wanted a pledge of no reprisals, told them that the government would decide what terms to accept, not any political
party.

But Casado, saying, "I can get much more out of Franco
than Negrín can," planned to take over the reins of the fal-
tering Republic himself. The stage was now set for the war
to end as it began—with a military revolt.

Casado won support from officers who were alarmed by
Negrín's appointment of Communists to key military com-
mands, especially that of the port city of Cartagena. On
March 5 coastal artillery units in Cartagena revolted, aided
by the Fifth Column, which emerged shouting "Long live
Franco." The fleet, harbored at Cartagena, put out to sea
and did not return even after Loyalist troops put down the
rebellion a few hours later. Negrín sent a plane to bring
Casado and other officials from Madrid to Yeste, near Alicante, for a Cabinet meeting. Pleading ill health, but actually
fearing arrest, Casado, Miaja, and several others refused
to board the craft. That night, when the Cabinet broke off its
meeting for dinner, it heard rumors of a rebellion in Madrid.
Thinking it might be a false rumor spread by the Nationalist
radio, Negrín called Casado. "What is going on in Madrid,
General?" he asked. "What is going on in Madrid is that I
have rebelled," Casado answered. Shocked, Negrín asked,
"Against whom? Against me?" "Yes, against you," was the
reply. Negrín, realizing his government had simply disinte-
grated, did not try to counter the coup. With several of his
remaining supporters, almost all of them Communists, he
flew to Dakar in French West Africa and from there to exile
in France.

The Communists that remained were not willing to give up

so easily; they had spearheaded the Republic's resistance throughout the war and many had only joined the party because of its war record. Now, they resented leaving the fate of the Republic in the hands of defeatists and old-line officers like Casado. Communist-led army units marched on Madrid, held most of it by March 8, but by March 13 were defeated. Franco's forces watched the remnants of the Republican army tear itself apart in a struggle that cost 2,000 lives. The National Defense Council of the Casado forces proposed peace terms that included no reprisals, independence from foreign powers, respect for the army, and a grace period of twenty-five days to allow Loyalists to leave the country. When Franco's answer came, it was from a source that demonstrated the hidden strength of the Fifth Column: an artillery colonel in the Republican army told Casado he was Franco's representative in Madrid and offered to negotiate surrender terms.

Casado soon found out that he could do no more than Negrín in securing guarantees against reprisals. The Nationalists merely stated that they would be generous with those who were not leaders but "had through deception been drawn into the struggle." Considering the constant executions in the Nationalist zone, this fell far short of the required assurances against reprisals. When Casado's negotiators flew to Burgos on March 23, they found there was nothing to negotiate; the Nationalists simply presented them with instructions that the Republic's air force should fly to Nationalist airfields on the 25th and that two days later all army commanders must cross over to rebel lines with papers showing the exact placement of their forces. While Casado's council busied itself with requesting minor changes in this arrangement, the first deadline passed and the Nationalists refused to talk any more.

On the 26th Franco's forces began marching, and the Caudillo went on the radio to announce that he wanted the immediate surrender of all armed Republicans. His troops faced no opposition. The Republican army simply dropped its weapons and left the field. Soldiers spontaneously took to the roads, walking home after nearly three years of war. In the Casa de Campo in Madrid haggard defenders and triumphant rebels were hugging each other with relief. From his plane, escaping to Valencia, Casado looked down on roads clogged with retreating soldiers. Everywhere, the Fifth Column was emerging from its hiding place, taking over the major cities even before the arrival of Nationalist troops. Republicans flocked to ports in search of ships to carry them to safety, but the ships never came. Some committed suicide then and there; others were rounded up by Falange killer squads; and still others were herded together with returning Republican soldiers to the open-air prisons of the bull-rings to await trial, imprisonment, and death.

On March 31 an aide informed General Franco that his armies were in total control of the entire country. "Very good," he sniffed through his head cold, "many thanks." The next day, April 1, he issued a simple statement: "Today, after capturing and disarming the Red Army, the National troops have attained their last military objectives. The War is over." On the same day, the United States recognized the Franco regime and Pope Pius XII sent a wire expressing "sincere thanks with your excellency for Spain's Catholic victory."

The New Spain's moment of glory came on May 19, when a parade of 120,000 Nationalist troops, sixteen miles long, marched in the Fascist goose step past an honor stand containing Franco, diplomats, generals, and churchmen. Flanking the stand were enormous columns, each with Franco's name repeated three times. Overhead, 500 planes flew in formation. The streets were filled with joyous throngs shouting the now-familiar chant: "Fran-co, Fran-co, Fran-co." Other Madrileños stayed behind closed doors at home, weeping for their fallen dead or for relatives who were filling Spain's prisons to overflowing.

The thousand-day-long agony of the Spanish Republic was over. One of the Two Spains had emerged victorious. The Spanish earth was blood-soaked; its cities in shambles, its people hungry. Spain's civil war had finally ended.

# 14

# *The Victor's Peace*

When Claude Bowers, the American ambassador to Spain and a strong supporter of the Republic, arrived at the White House for a meeting with President Roosevelt in March 1939, the President's first words were: "We have made a mistake; you have been right all along."

The mistake was to let the Spanish Republic die. It was the legal, elected government of Spain, one that embodied the hopes and aspirations of the people to a greater degree than most governments of the Depression-shattered world of the 1930's. The Republic was sacrificed to an appeasement policy that failed. Because they feared to anger Hitler, Britain and France neglected their basic self-interests in the Spanish peninsula and cut off aid to a potential ally, ensuring its defeat. The Russians, after frustrating years of trying to persuade the democracies to help the Republic and to form a collective security agreement against Germany, finally gave up, and in July 1939 allied themselves with Hitler in an attempt to buy time before the Germans turned upon them.

Five months after the civil war ended, Europe went up in flames. Hitler's limitless ambitions could no longer be satisfied by conference-table victories. Lulled by the easy agreement of France and England to dismember the Czech state at Munich, and by their refusal to aid the Spanish Republic, he did not think they would fight when German troops marched into Poland in September 1939. The conflagration spread, and the world was at war. This sequence of events justified Negrín's strategy of holding out in the hope that the democracies would finally come to their senses and make a stand, but it was too late to save the Republic.

It was too late also for the hundreds of thousands of Spanish refugees stranded in camps in southern France. It was too late for the dead, the wounded, the political prisoners in Spain. Once Germany and Italy intervened in the civil war, it became the first great battle of what was to become the Second World War. It was in Spain that forces representing the warring political ideologies of the 1930's— democracy, communism, and fascism—first met in armed combat.

The people of London, Coventry, and Rotterdam were to feel the weight of bombs and fires in terror raids on civilians that were first felt by the Spaniards of Madrid, Guernica, and Barcelona. The German tank tactics that punched holes in the Republican lines in the Aragon offensive were repeated against the French in 1940, when massed armor sped through supposedly invincible positions. The military lessons of the Spanish training grounds were used by the Germans as they conquered most of Europe, helped by war materials from their officially neutral allies in Nationalist Spain.

Despite the involvement of foreign powers, the civil war was a uniquely Spanish affair at the outset. Mutual antagonisms that had hardened over past generations finally exploded in a paroxysm of bloodletting in 1936. The Germans and Italians helped transform a straightforward military conspiracy into a totalitarian state complete with the trappings of fascism. The Russians helped transform a liberal Republic into a dependent state that was forced to follow Moscow's bidding and had to swallow the indignities inflicted by Stalin's secret police.

Spain's civil war left it torn and bleeding. Spain was a poor country when the war began; at its end it was destitute. It took the better part of two decades for the country to recover. The material damage was awesome—half a million buildings destroyed or damaged, 183 towns all but ruined, a third of the livestock in the country lost. The human losses were even more appalling. Nearly 300,000 men died on the battlefields; another 200,000 probably died in the terror campaigns behind the lines, the vast majority of them in the Nationalist zone; and it has been estimated that 200,000 or more died from malnutrition and disease as a result of wartime conditions and the post-war famine.

Had Franco embarked on a Lincolnesque policy of "malice toward none; with charity for all," the country still would have gone through a terrible ordeal. But the peace that descended on the battlefields did not end the slaughter. The victors treated their former enemies, not as people who were wrong and who now must be welcomed back into the fold, but as a cancer that had to be cut out of Spain by drastic surgery. Huge concentration camps were set up immediately after the war ended, and at least 300,000 people were held while their "crimes" were investigated. As they were found guilty and either killed or sent to prison for terms that ranged up to thirty years, others replaced them; one estimate is that two million people were held for at least some time in the Nationalists' prisons and concentration camps.

Trials for offenses under the Law of Political Responsibility were drumhead courts-martial dispensing vengeance rather than justice. Count Ciano wrote during a visit to Spain in July 1939 that he found "trials going on every day at a speed which I would almost call summary. . . . There are still a great number of shootings. In Madrid alone between 200 and 250 a day, in Barcelona, 150, and in Seville, a city that was never in the hands of the Reds, 80." In 1944 a Nationalist official leaked a report to an American newsman that stated 192,684 people had been executed since the end of the war. These official murders were only ended after it became clear that Hitler would lose the war and Franco decided it would be in his best interests to moderate the excesses of his regime to improve relations with the democracies. Spain's prisons, bulging with political prisoners, were gradually emptied in a series of amnesties, and by 1964 few if any civil war victims were still in jail.

While Franco tightened his grip on Spain, the Republicans were in disarray. Some leading figures went to Russia, but most went to France or Mexico, where they maintained a Republic-in-exile and carried on an ineffective propaganda war against the Nationalists who had beaten them and the Communists who had betrayed them. Many died during World War II: Largo spent the war in a German concentration camp and died soon after its end; the Catalan leader Companys was among several Republicans handed over to Spain by the German puppet government in France and shot. Most of the high-ranking Russian officers fell victim to Stalin's purges when they returned home. The strong man of the prewar Republic, Azaña, died in France in 1940; the strong man of the wartime Republic, Negrín, died in Mexican exile in 1956. Some 70,000 refugees in French camps died of disease and hunger within the first three years following the end of the civil war, and many of those who fled to Russia died during the war of either wartime raids or hunger. The Loyalists in France supplied some 25,000 fighters for the Free French underground. The Americans of the Lincoln

Battalion found themselves branded with the Communist label and suffered discrimination in the armed forces during World War II and in the years of the Cold War anti-communism that followed. They often referred to themselves as "premature anti-Fascists" in that they fought fascism in Spain five years before it became fashionable to do so.

World War II found Spain officially neutral, too devastated by the civil war and the desperate food shortage to enter the war on the side of Germany. It is probable that the cautious Franco planned to stay out of the war until Germany was on the verge of victory and then enter it in order to make territorial claims on the French North African empire. That moment never came, and Hitler put tremendous pressure on Franco to allow German troops into Spain to take the British fortress of Gibraltar. Franco first pleaded that Spanish troops had to do the job alone, then said he feared the British would seize the Canary Islands, and finally made exorbitant demands on Germany, itself strained by wartime shortages, for food, oil, and arms. On October 23, 1940, the Führer met the stubborn Caudillo in a railway car at the French border town of Hendaye and was driven to fury by Franco's endless lecture on the war and world politics, delivered in a whining, high-pitched monotone that led Hitler to say later: "I would rather have three or four teeth pulled rather than meet that man again." Hitler sent Mussolini to talk Franco into the war, but the Italian, whose troops were bogged down in the Balkans, was asked "Duce, if you could get out of this war, would you?" To which Mussolini laughed, "You bet your life I would."

Spain's weakened condition, the pro-British sentiment in some sectors of the army, its fear of British counter-attack if it openly entered the war on Germany's side, and Franco's nationalism that made him fearful of letting German troops on Spain's soil combined to delay Spanish entry into the war. "You know how a thing will start, but not how it will end," Franco said, and he determined to keep Spain officially neutral, but with the option to join Hitler if he looked like a winner. In June 1941 Hitler turned on Russia, and this was an aspect of the war Franco could support wholeheartedly. In July he sent a "volunteer" force, the "Blue Division," to fight in Russia under German command. Almost 50,000 Spaniards served on the Russian front, and more than 6,000 were killed helping Hitler's attempt to conquer Soviet Russia. Another 15,000 Spanish workmen were sent to labor in German war factories, and the Germans rounded up about 40,000 Spanish Republican exiles in occupied France and shipped them to forced labor in Germany.

After the Germans were defeated at Stalingrad in January 1943, Franco concluded that Hitler would lose the war and began trimming his sails to adjust to a post-war world dominated by the United States and England. Executions tapered off, his neutrality became more vocal, and he reshuffled his Cabinet to include more pro-British officers and diplomats. Pro-Nazi propaganda was muted, and Franco told everyone who would listen that he wasn't against the democracies, only against the Russians.

At the war's end in 1945 Spain was set apart from the world's community of nations. In 1946 the United Nations reported: "In origin, nature, structure and general conduct the Franco regime is a Fascist regime patterned on, and established largely as a result of aid received from Hitler's Germany and Mussolini's Fascist Italy." Spain was excluded from the UN, which recommended that countries withdraw their ambassadors from Madrid. The UN's action gave heart to the Republican exiles who thought it was the prelude to Franco's downfall, and Communist-led guerrilla actions mounted within Spain. But the foreign pressures boomeranged as even those Spaniards who disliked Franco were insulted by what they considered foreign intervention in Spain's internal affairs. Franco was able to appeal to Spain's strong nationalism to counter the pressures from without.

As both the civil war and the world war faded from memory, to be replaced by a Cold War between the western democracies and Communist Russia, Spain slowly re-entered the family of nations. The United States concluded a military alliance in 1953, exchanging cash and aid for military bases; Spain finally entered the United Nations in 1955; and the tight hold of Franco's dictatorship gradually lessened as the country's economy improved and as internal resistance faded. The personality cult that had plastered Franco's portrait on the walls and shop windows of Spain was ended, and the trappings of fascism that had marked the early years of the Nationalist regime were dropped. Franco's aim was to de-politicize Spain, to create a nation of order, free from political factionalism. "Every people is haunted by its familiar demons," the Caudillo told the powerless Cortes in 1966, "and Spain's are an anarchistic spirit, negativism, lack of solidarity, extremism, and mutual hostility." It was to scourge these demons that the dictatorship killed and imprisoned so many Spaniards, and, as it mellowed with time, replaced overt oppression with more subtle means of control to keep the ghosts of Spain in the shadows.

General Franco was maintained in power for well over thirty years by more than the bayonets of the Guardias or the war-weariness of the population. He proved himself an extraordinarily adroit politician for one who professed a hatred of politics. He learned the delicate art of balancing differing interests and political forces in the desert wars of Morocco where he bargained with the local sultans and tribal chiefs. As Caudillo of Spain he followed similar tactics: bribery in the form of government jobs, symbolic gestures, or economic favoritism won otherwise contending factions to his side; for those who clung to opposition, the velvet glove was taken off, revealing the iron fist of imprisonment or forced exile.

Franco artfully manipulated his supporters—the army, the Falange, the Monarchists, big business, and the Church— and crushed his enemies. The army, which supported him from the beginning, supplied top advisers and Cabinet ministers, and was kept happy by modernization programs carried out with American military aid. The Falange was bought with government jobs and lip-service to Falangist ideals of the corporate state, and its extremists checked by the power of the army. Big business was kept loyal through policies that kept labor cheap and plentiful, favored large profits, and turned over the economy to economic technicians whose policies fostered growth and expansion. Although many Monarchists thought the end of the civil war would bring restoration of the royal family, Franco dashed their hopes, insisting on continued military rule while holding out the prospects for an eventual royalist Spain. Finally, in 1969, Franco announced that Juan Carlos, the grandson of King Alfonso, who was deposed in 1931, would become king of Spain at his death.

The Church welcomed Franco as the savior who had rescued Spain from revolution and was a strong supporter of the regime until a newer, more liberal generation of clerics, influenced by the teachings of Pope John XXIII, became vocal in protesting the continuing poverty of the masses of people and the regime's dictatorial methods. In the 1960's a number of high churchmen condemned Spain's social inequality, and in 1971 an assembly of the country's bishops and priests declared: "We humbly recognize, and ask pardon for it, that we failed at the proper time to be ministers of reconciliation in the midst of our people, divided by a war between brothers." Franco quickly clamped down, ordering churchmen to confine themselves to "spiritual matters," but the Church is no longer the reactionary barrier to Spain's progress that it was in the 1930's.

The tensions that divided Spain and led to a bloody civil war have been suppressed but they still exist, and in some cases have deepened. The economic progress made in the past decade or so has not resulted in sharply lessened poverty. Nearly a million Spaniards are still exported to the factories of western Europe because they can't find work in their homeland. The tourist boom that paved over southern farmland with hotels turned farmers and fishermen into busboys and waiters, replacing their way of life but leaving their poverty intact. Growing industrialization has brought about a massive internal migration from the land to the cities, and the newly urbanized workers have often asserted their right to strike in defiance of government bans. These changes have even penetrated the most conservative areas of Spain, and in 1973 the old Carlist stronghold of Pamplona was shaken by a strike of 2,000 workers that won public support and sympathy strikes by 18,000 other workers in the city. Catalonia and the Basque region are once more centers of dissent. In Catalonia the government's attempts to supress the Catalan language and customs have failed, and the popular national dance, the *sardana*, is seen in the streets of Barcelona at every occasion as a veiled form of political statement. The Basques suffered severe repression after the war, but still use their outlawed language, and Basque guerrillas have increased their activities in recent years. In December 1973 they assassinated Premier Luis Carrero Blanco.

The Catholic political leader Gil Robles said he did not want to impose a dictatorship in the 1930's because Primo de Rivera's dictatorship had led to the fall of the king and "a new dictatorship could produce, after a period of tranquillity, social revolution." It is possible that after the awkward transition period following Franco's departure from the scene, Spain may yet go through another convulsion of social revolution. The outward stability is deceptive, for the accumulated hatreds and injustices of nearly forty years of dictatorship might erupt into a repetition of the upheavals of the 1930's. The heir-apparent, Juan Carlos, is often jokingly referred to as "Juan the Brief." Most Spaniards were born after the end of the civil war and are less influenced by the issues that swirled about an older Spain than they are by the secular, modernizing world of today. Franco's long effort to stifle dissent, to end political independence, and to maintain an authoritarian state may be doomed to ultimate failure, just as Spain's traditional morality is giving way to the inroads made by scantily clad Swedish and American tourists and its economy has responded to the demands of international trade and the European Common Market.

But it is also possible that the structure of Spanish authoritarianism will survive such changes, that its combination of economic progress, mild police control of dissent, and rule by a military-industrial complex will prove able to adapt to the world of the 1970's and 1980's. It fits a pattern that has developed in many other nations that lack democratic traditions, and even in some that still think of themselves as democracies.

The old battlefields are quiet now. The dead sleep beneath the Spanish earth. Olive trees grow where trenches and barbed wire once scratched the soil. Visitors to the National Palace in

Madrid can still see bullet holes in the ceilings of the royal chambers, but outside, the grassy slopes of the Casa de Campo are green again and a new University City has risen on the ashes of the old. The roads on which hundreds of thousands of refugees fled Málaga and Barcelona with their few possessions on their backs or on handcarts are super-highways today, flanked by skyscraper hotels for the more than twenty million foreign tourists who yearly flock to Spain's sunny shores.

The hatreds of the past still smolder in the hearts of many, and the symbols of the past are everywhere: every city has its Avenida José Antonio de Primo de Rivera and its Plaza Calvo Sotelo. But the symbol of modern Spain is an enormous crypt carved into the mountains some thirty miles northwest of Madrid, near the palace-museum of the Escorial. It is the Valley of the Fallen, a "temple of the dead" to shelter the remains of those who died on both sides of the war. Chiseled into the side of a mountain is a huge basilica of granite and marble, large enough for 10,000 people to assemble behind its bronze doors that weigh eleven tons each. Atop the mountain is a granite cross thrusting five hundred feet into the air, which can be seen for many miles and which, floodlit, dominates the valley at night. Meant as a tribute to the fallen dead and a symbol of Spain's new-found unity, this modern equivalent of the pharaoh's pyramids was built with the slave labor of Republican prisoners of war. Started in 1942, it was not finished until 1958, and it stands now as a reminder of the gruesome civil war that left close to a million Spaniards dead, and gravely wounded the hopes and dreams of people the world over who saw in Spain's struggle a contest between good and evil which elevated a national tragedy to a symbolic encounter that had profound meaning for all men, everywhere.

Perhaps the ultimate meaning of that terrible war, the symbolic element in that conflict which gives it a universality of meaning whose impact remains strong decades after the last shot was fired, was revealed by the French philosopher and novelist Albert Camus, who wrote: "It was in Spain that men learned that one can be right and yet be beaten, that force can vanquish spirit, that there are times when courage is not its own recompense. It is this, doubtless, which explains why so many men, the world over, feel the Spanish drama as a personal tragedy."

# Books for Further Reading

Bolloten, Burnett, *The Grand Camouflage: The Spanish Civil War and Revolution, 1936–39*. New York: Frederick A. Praeger, 1961.

Borkenau, Franz, *The Spanish Cockpit: An Eyewitness Account of the Political and Social Conflicts of the Spanish Civil War*. Ann Arbor: University of Michigan Press, 1963.

Brenan, Gerald, *The Spanish Labyrinth*. New York: Cambridge University Press, 1960.

Carr, Raymond, ed., *The Republic and the Civil War in Spain*. New York: St. Martin's Press, 1971.

Cattell, David T., *Communism and the Spanish Civil War*. New York: Russell and Russell, 1965.

Colodny, Robert Garland, *The Struggle for Madrid: The Central Epic of the Spanish Conflict (1936–37)*. New York: Paine-Whitman, 1958.

Jackson, Gabriel, *The Spanish Republic and the Civil War, 1931–1939*. Princeton: Princeton University Press, 1965.

Malefakis, Edward E., *Agrarian Reform and Peasant Revolution in Spain: Origins of the Civil War*. New Haven: Yale University Press, 1970.

Orwell, George, *Homage to Catalonia*. New York: Harcourt, Brace, 1952.

Payne, Robert, ed., *The Civil War in Spain, 1936–39*. New York: G. P. Putnam's Sons, 1962.

Payne, Stanley G., *Politics and the Military in Modern Spain*. Stanford: Stanford University Press, 1967.

Puzzo, Dante A., *Spain and the Great Powers, 1936–1941*. New York: Columbia University Press, 1962.

Rosenstone, Robert A., *Crusade on the Left: The Lincoln Battallion in the Spanish Civil War.* New York: Pegasus, 1970.

Sánchez, José M., *Reform and Reaction: The Politico-Religious Background of the Spanish Civil War.* Chapel Hill: University of North Carolina Press, 1964.

Thomas, Hugh, *The Spanish Civil War.* New York: Harper & Row, 1961.

Trythall, J. W. D., *El Caudillo: A Political Biography of Franco.* New York: McGraw-Hill, 1970.

# *Index*